I am Tom, an

MW01396630

My name is____________________

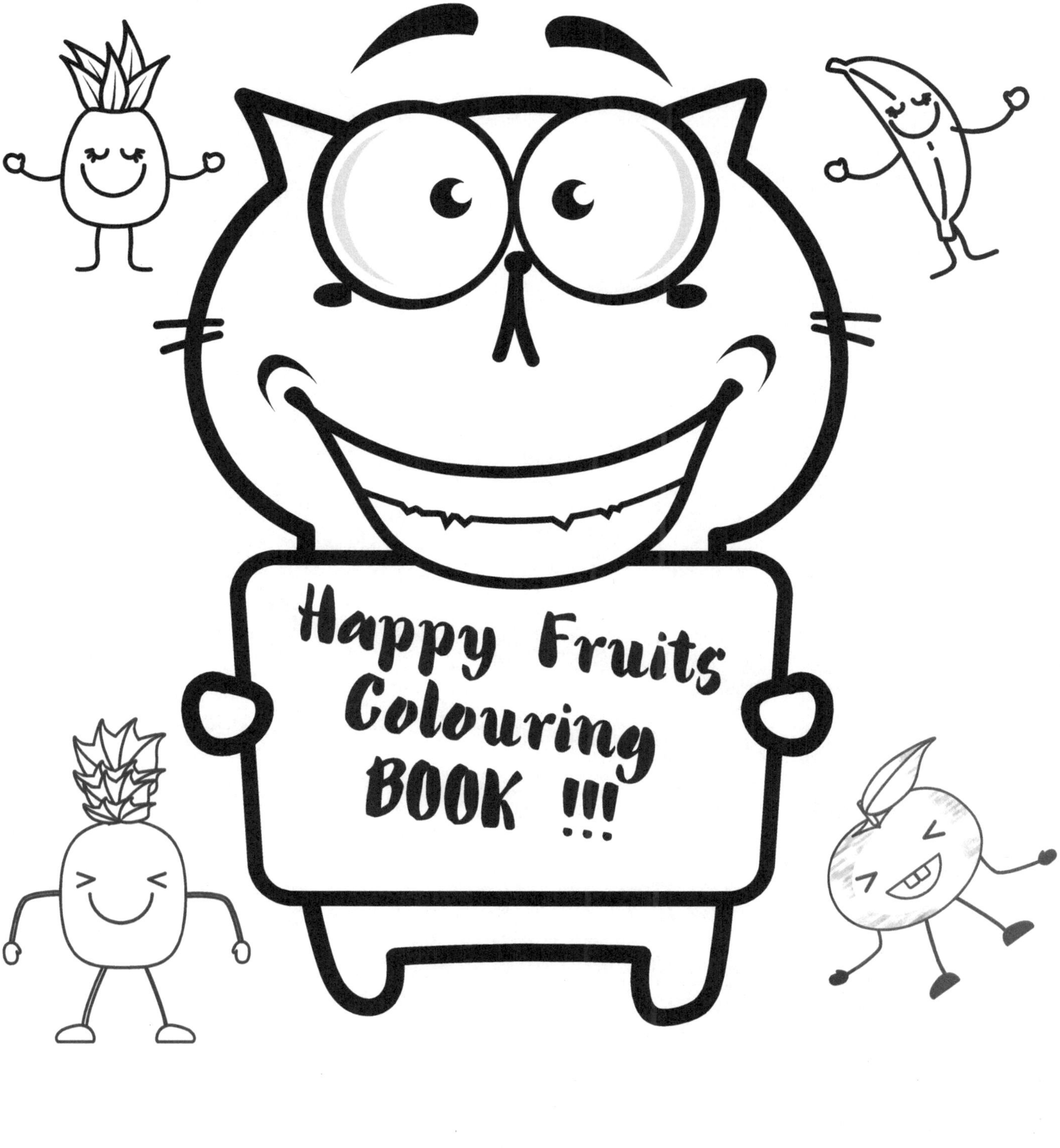

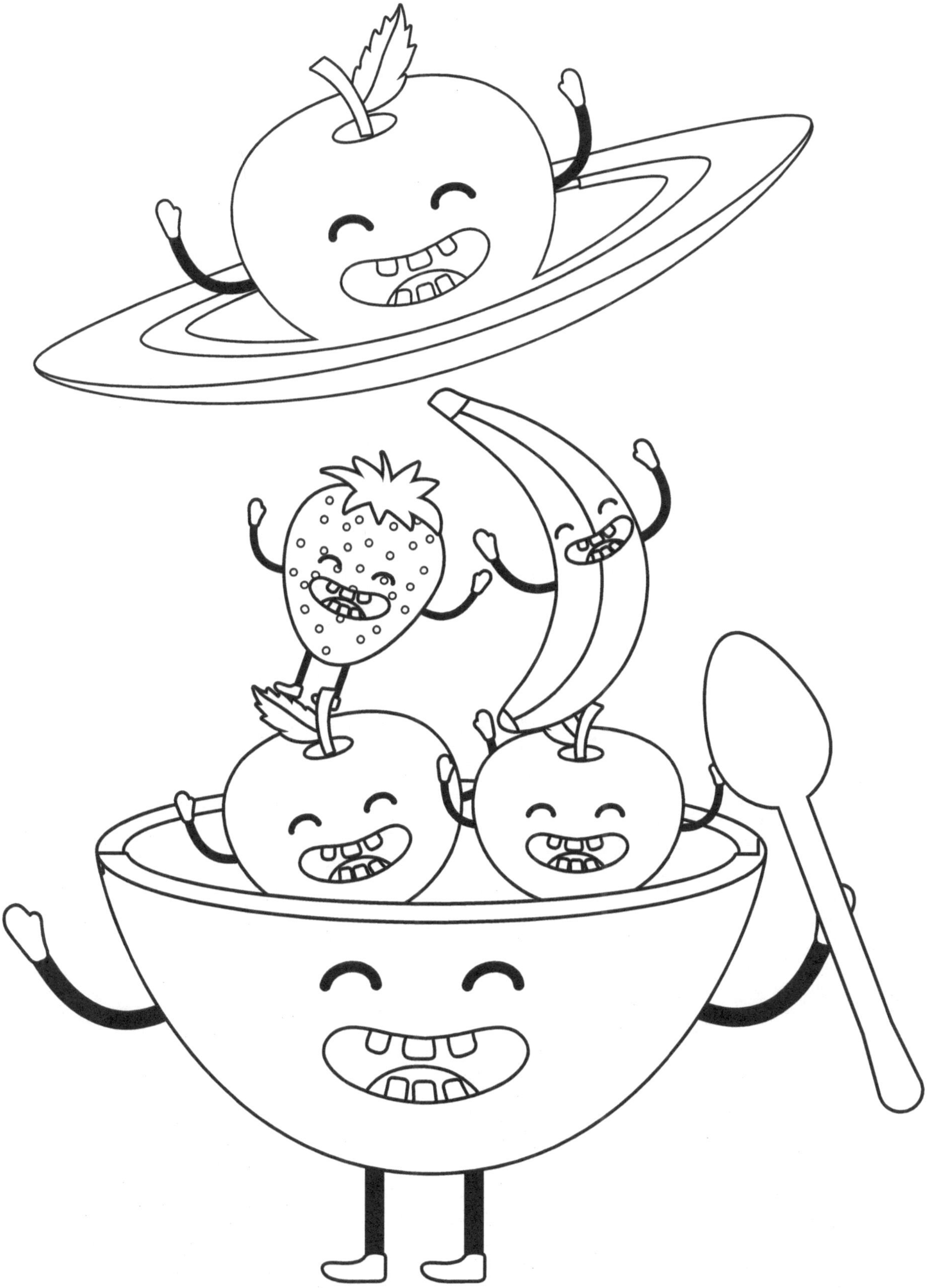

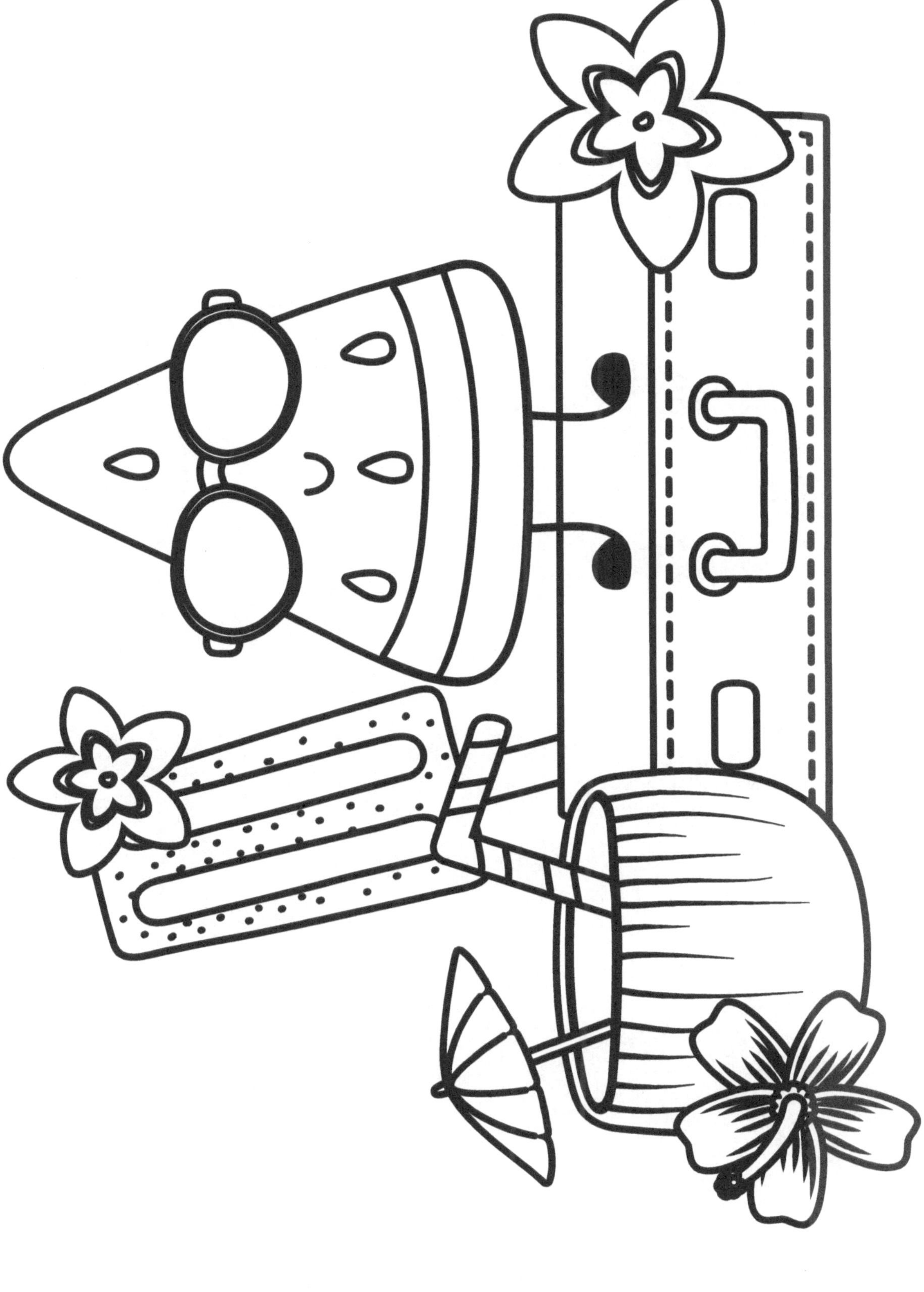

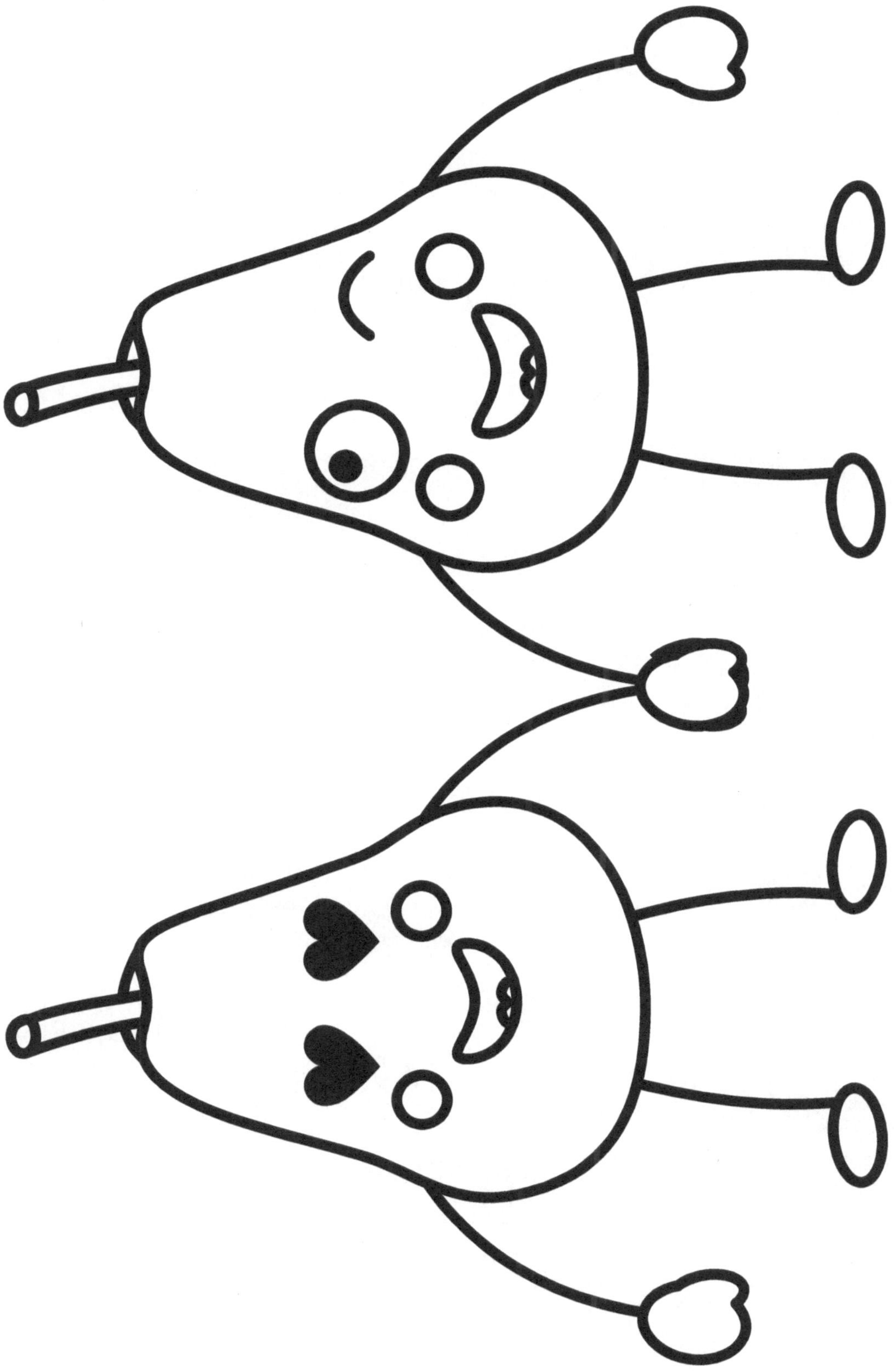

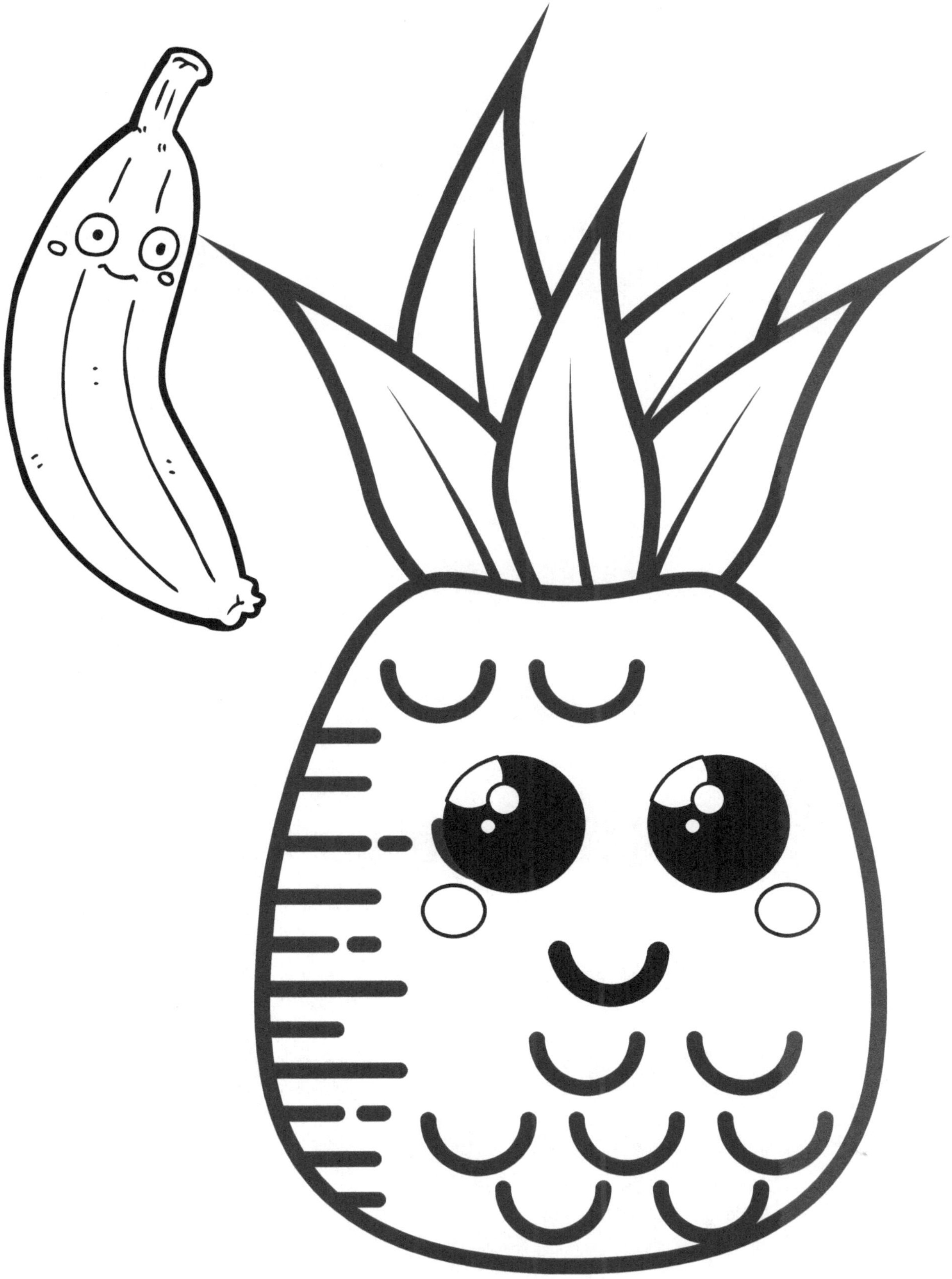

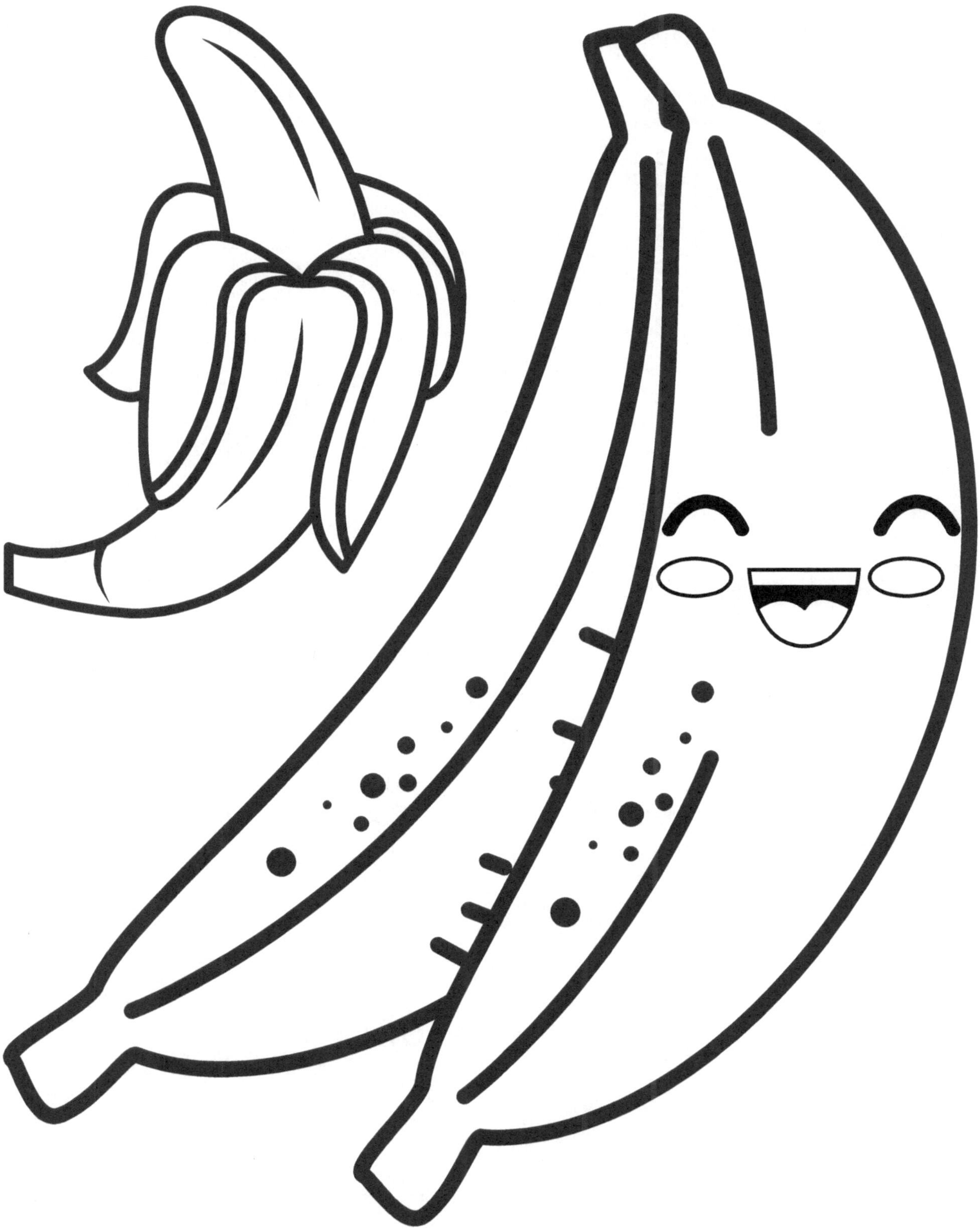

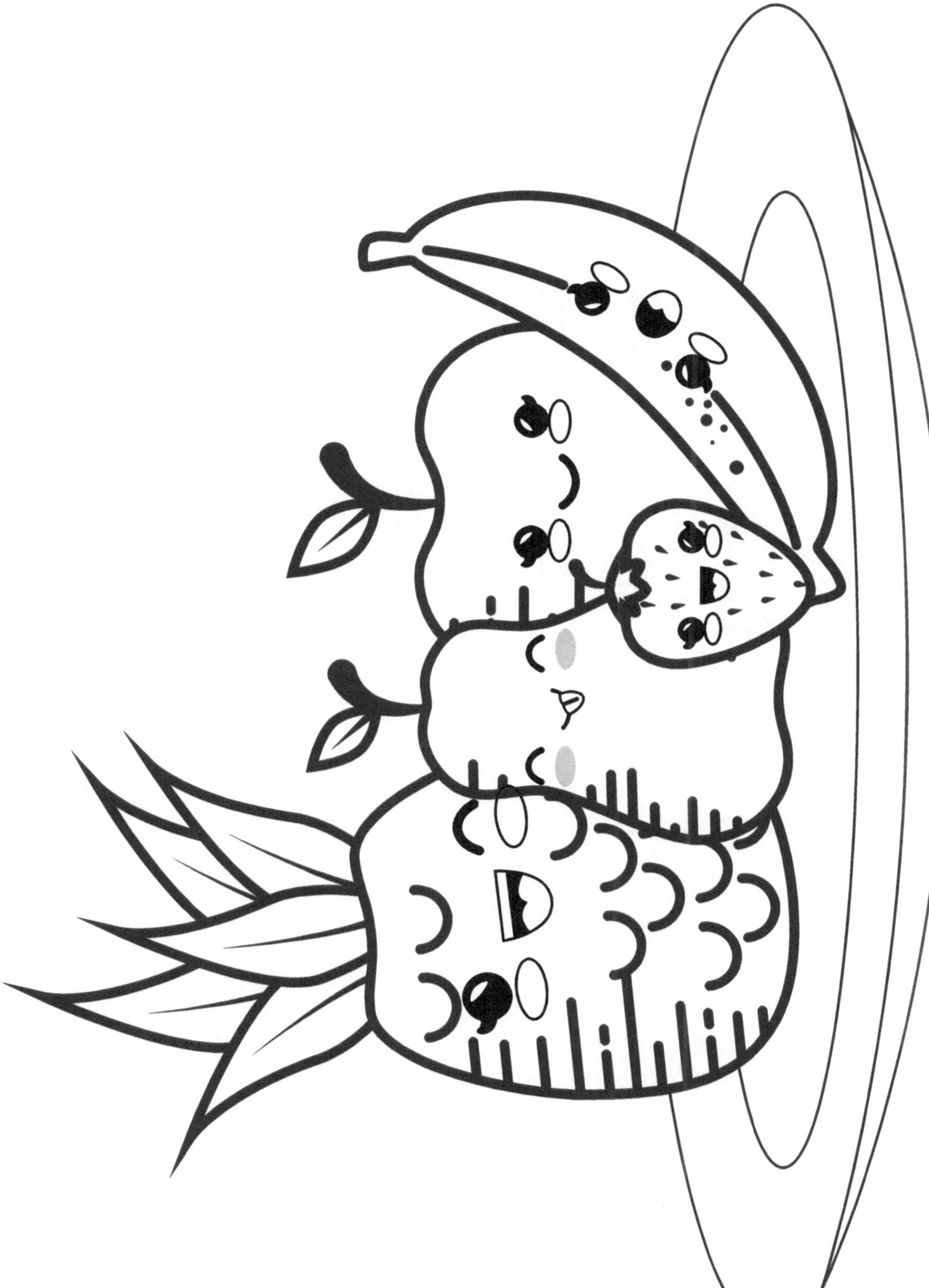

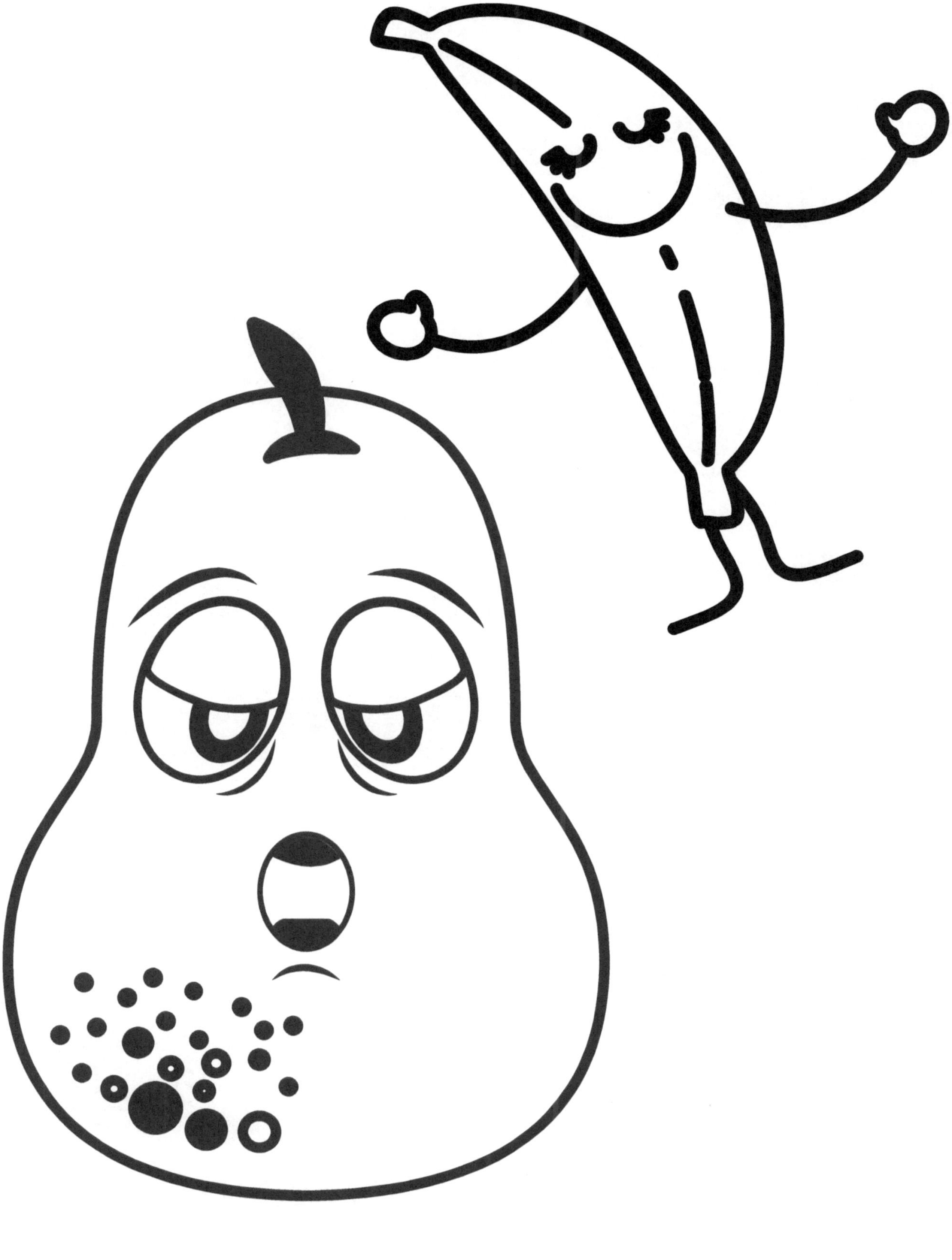

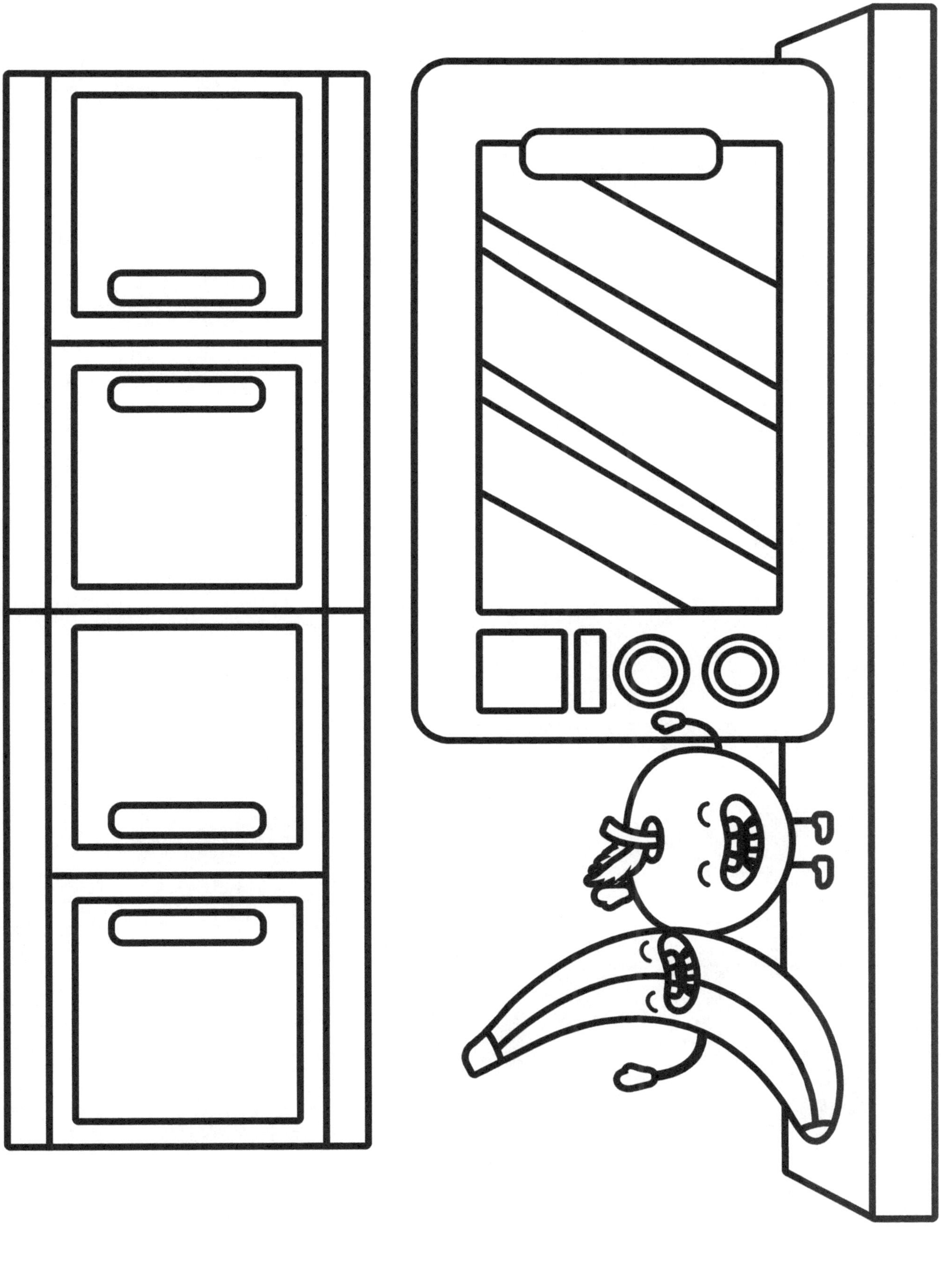

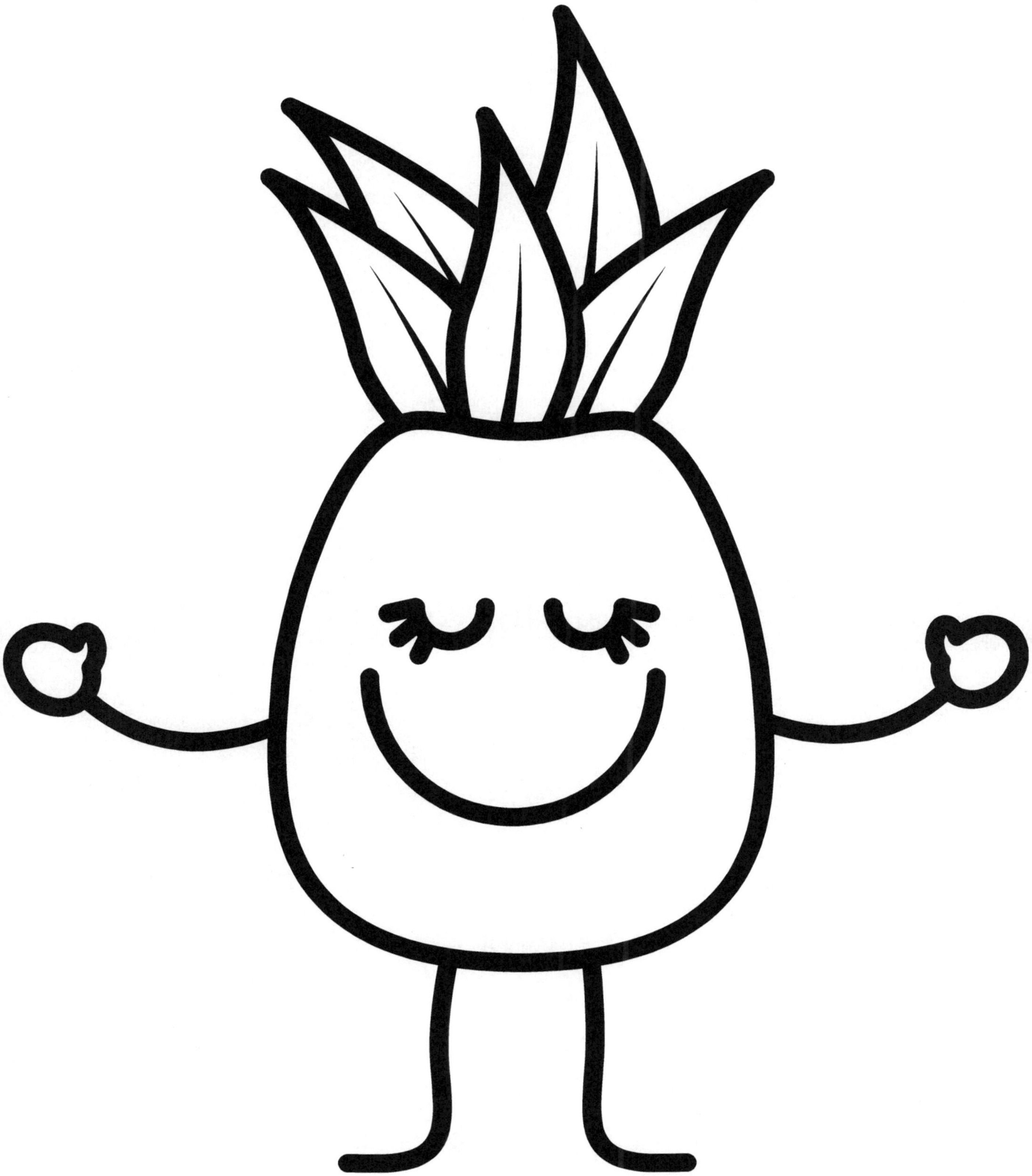

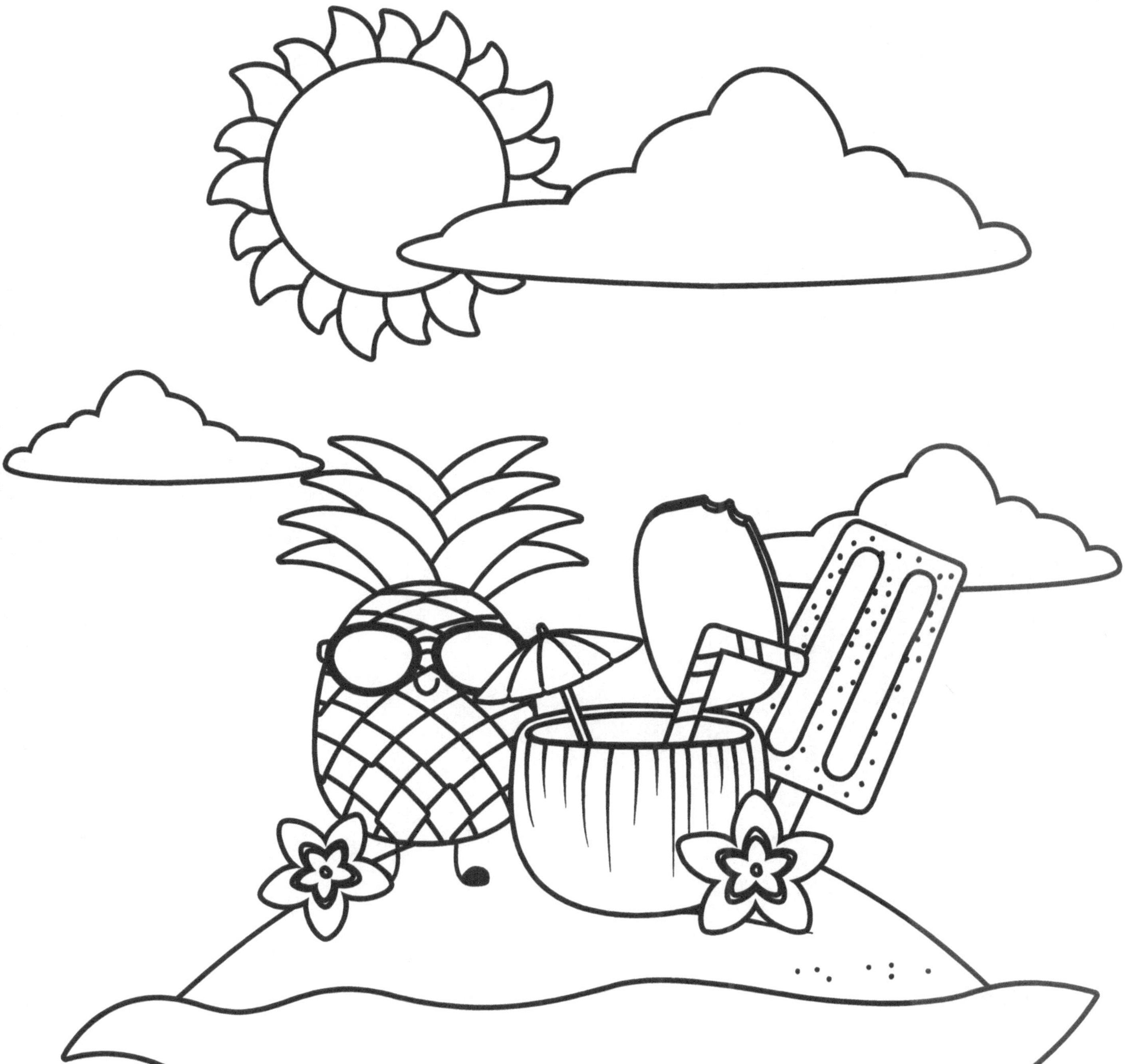

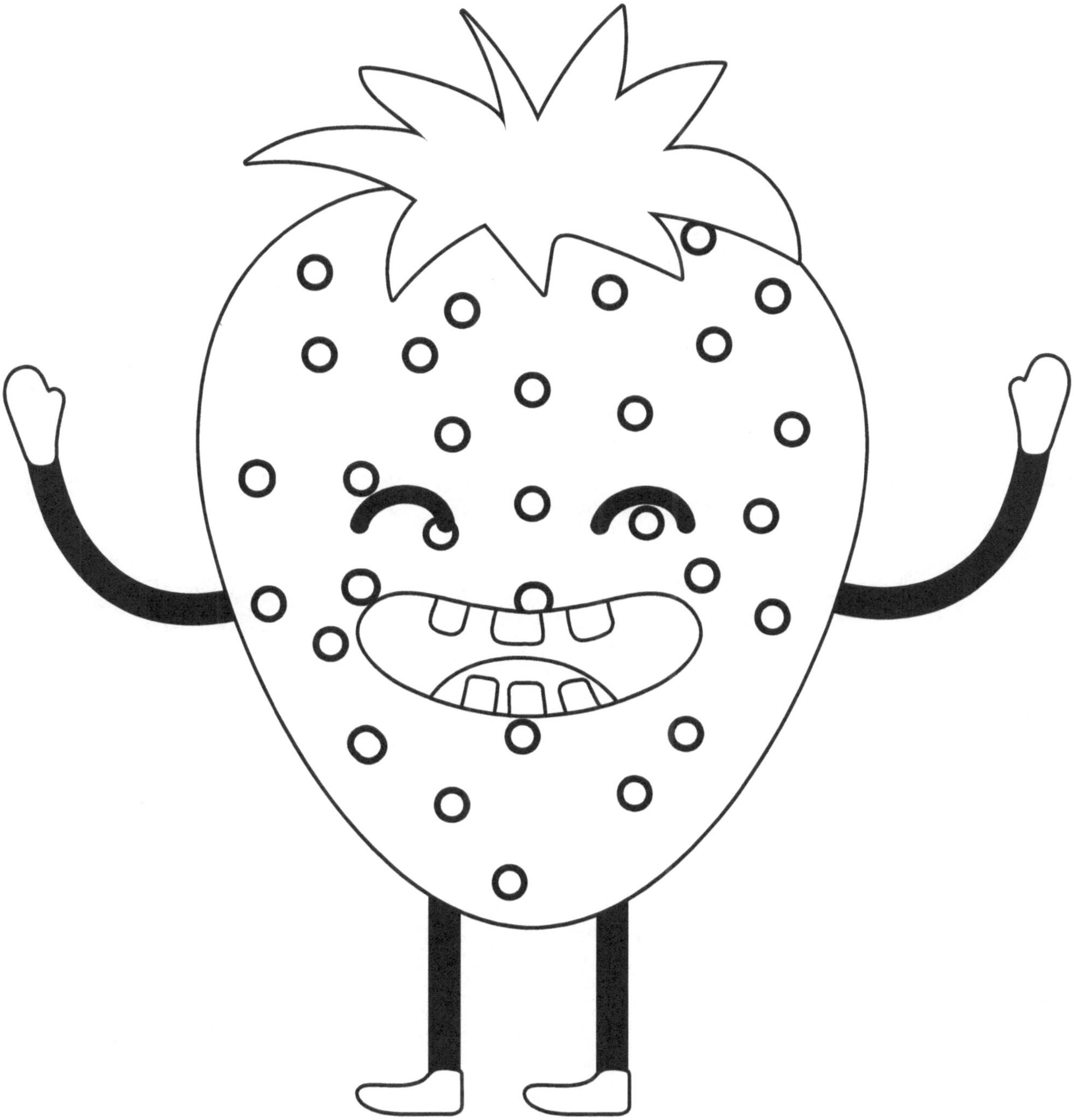

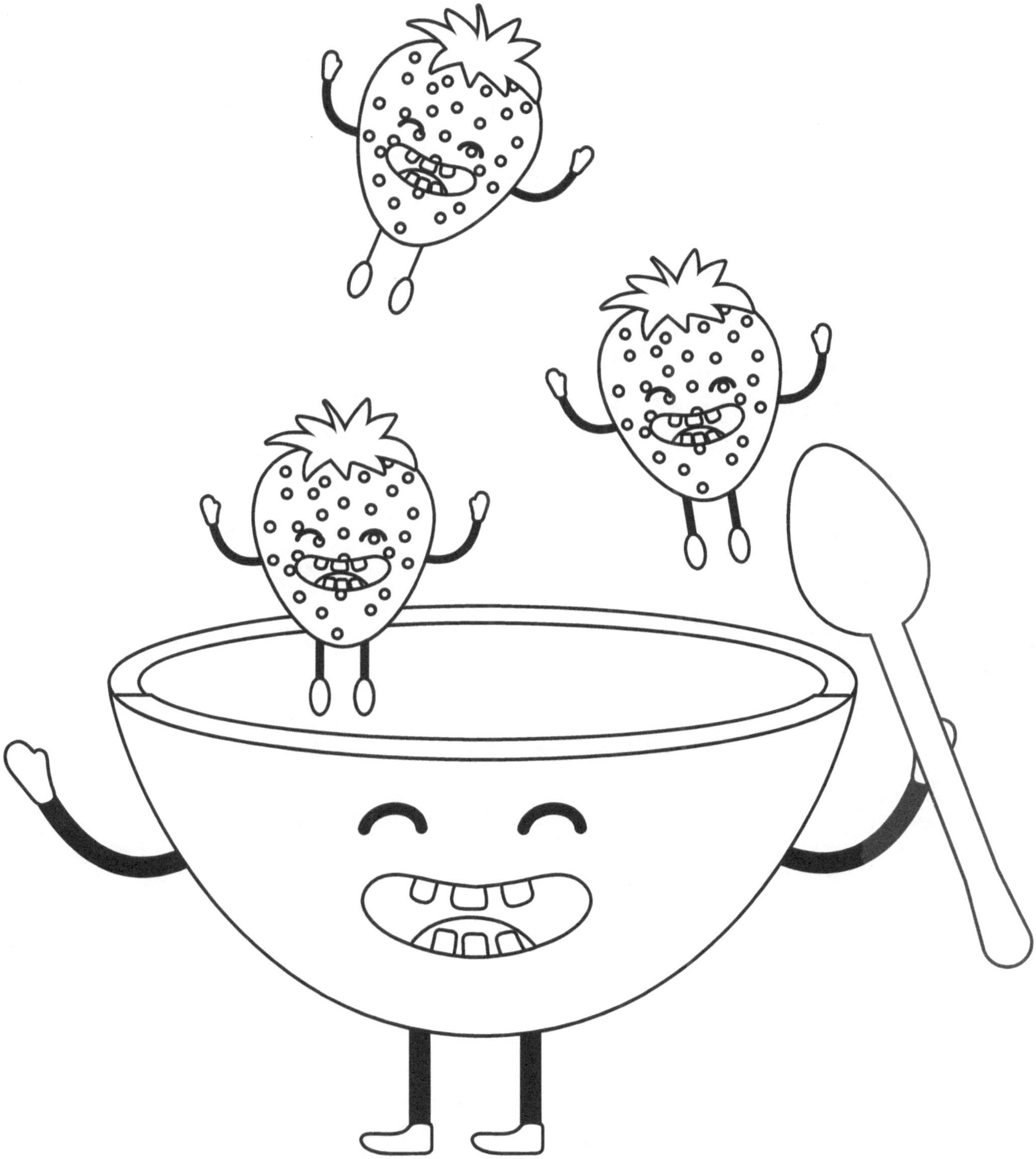

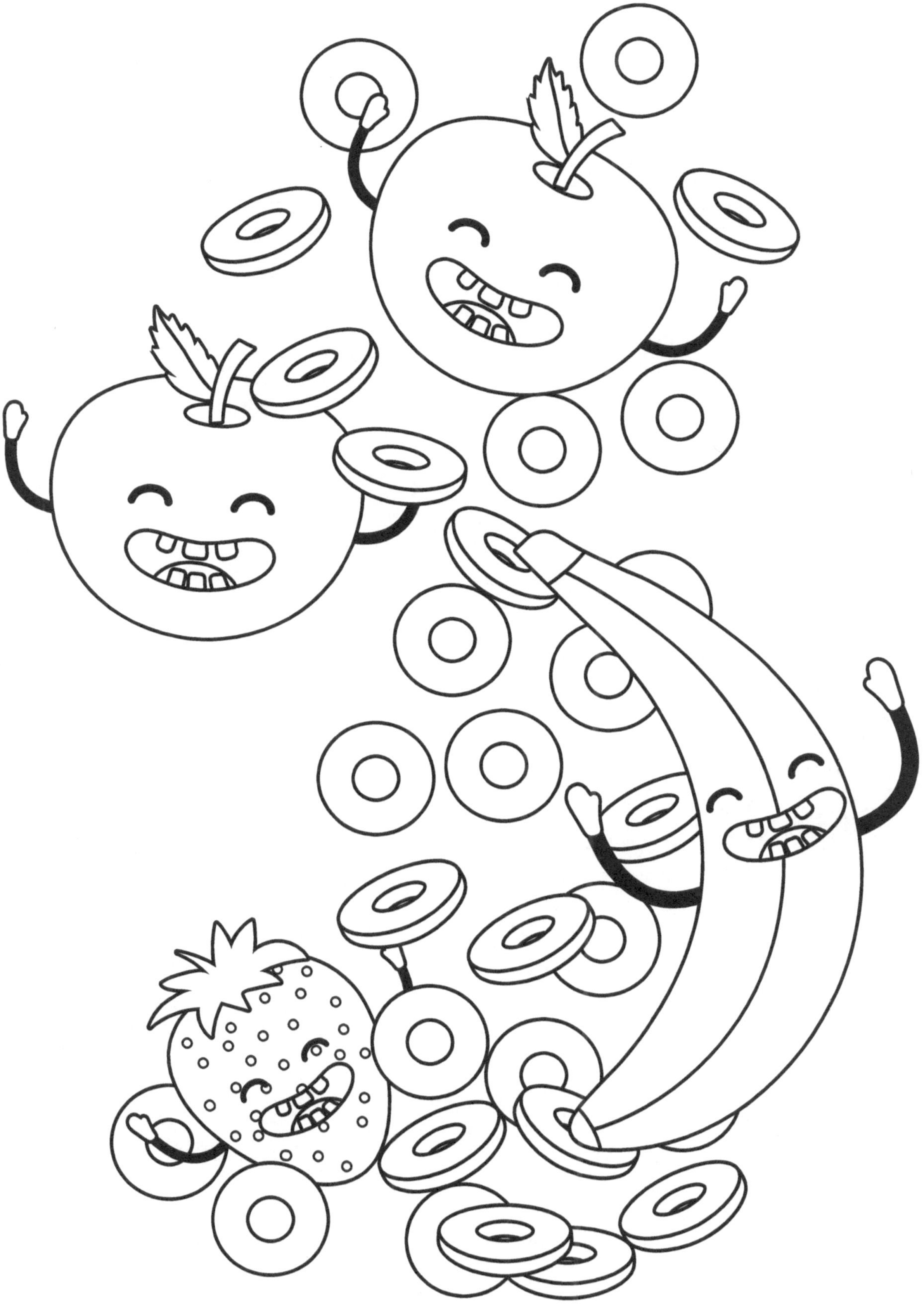

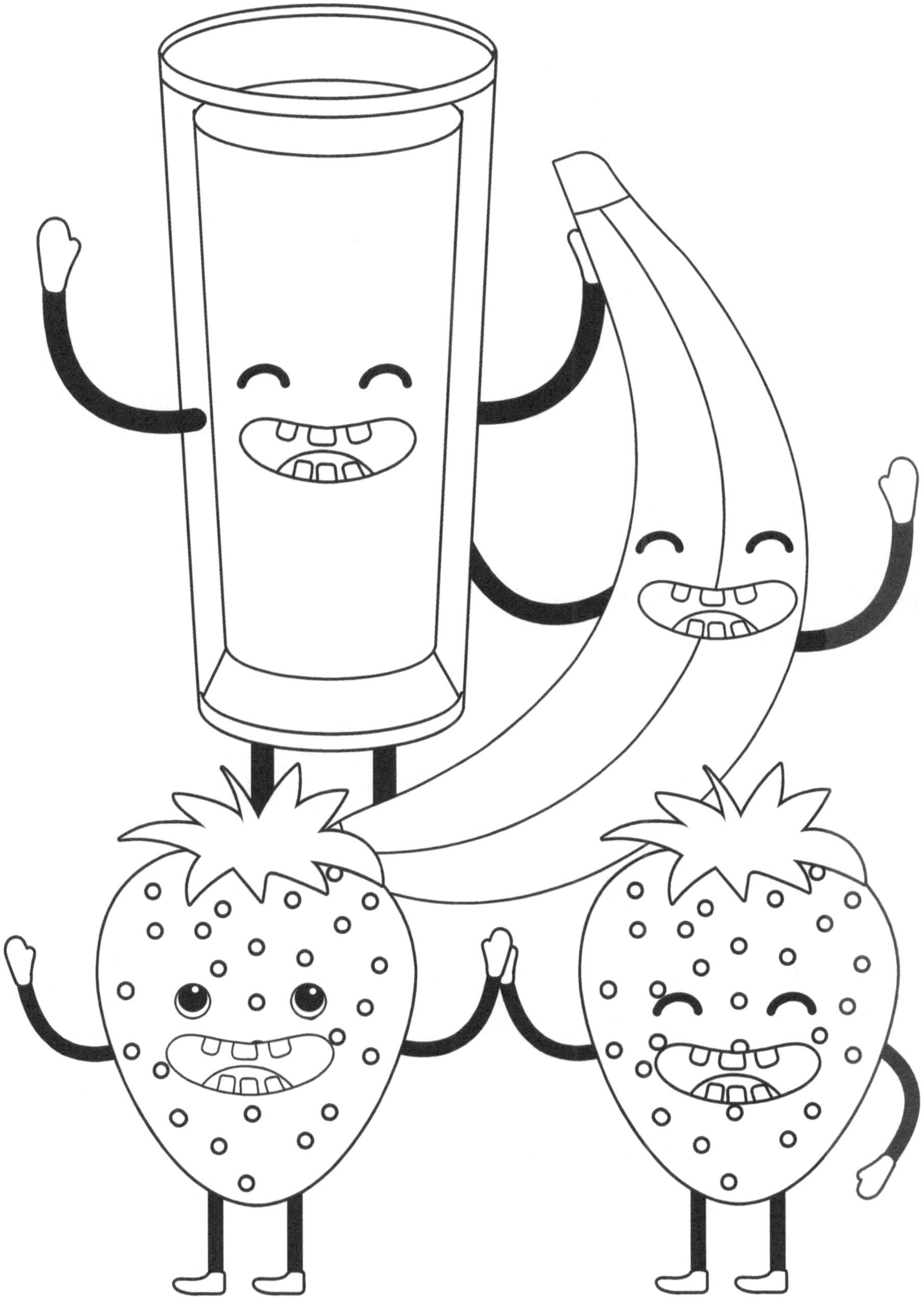

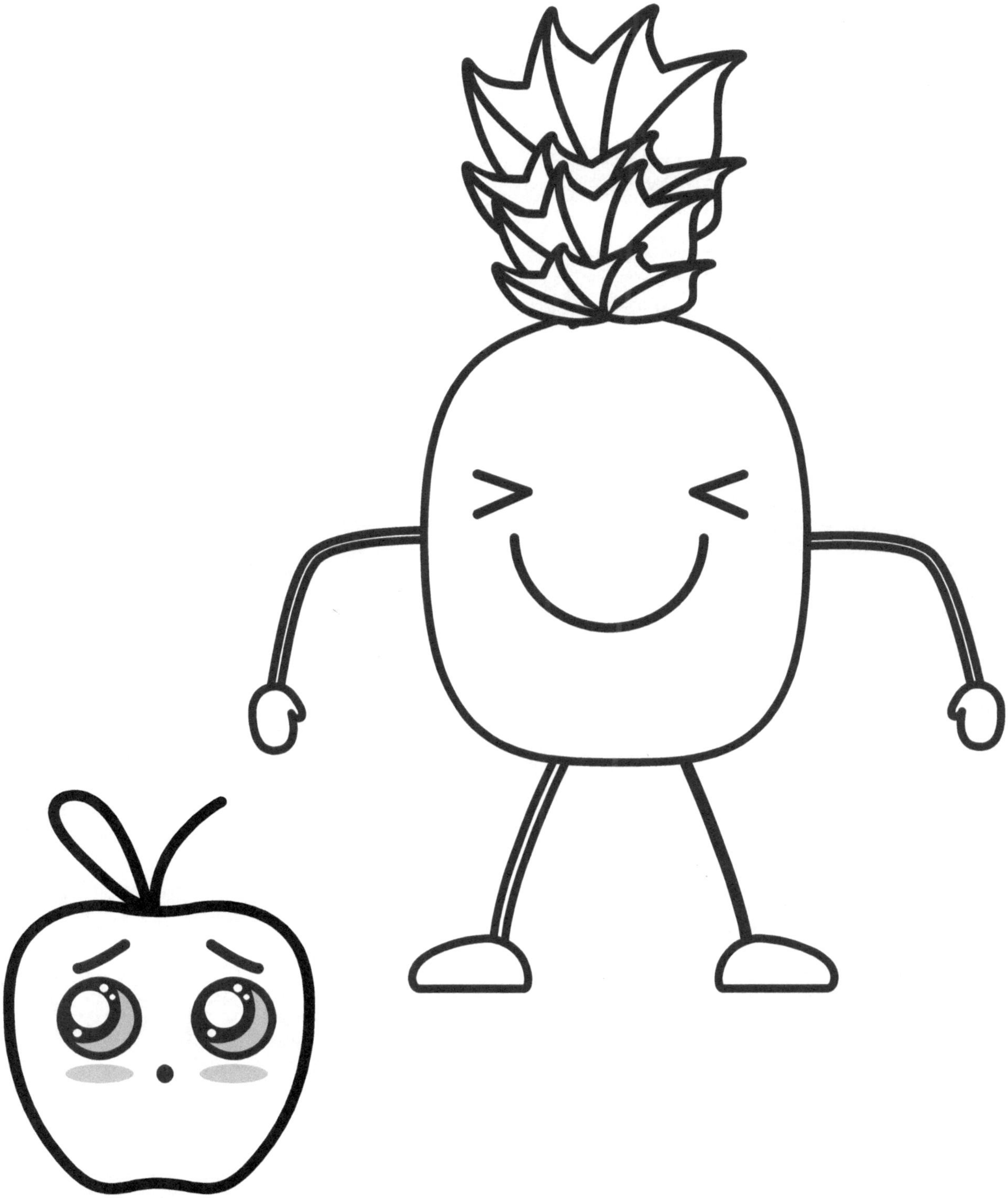

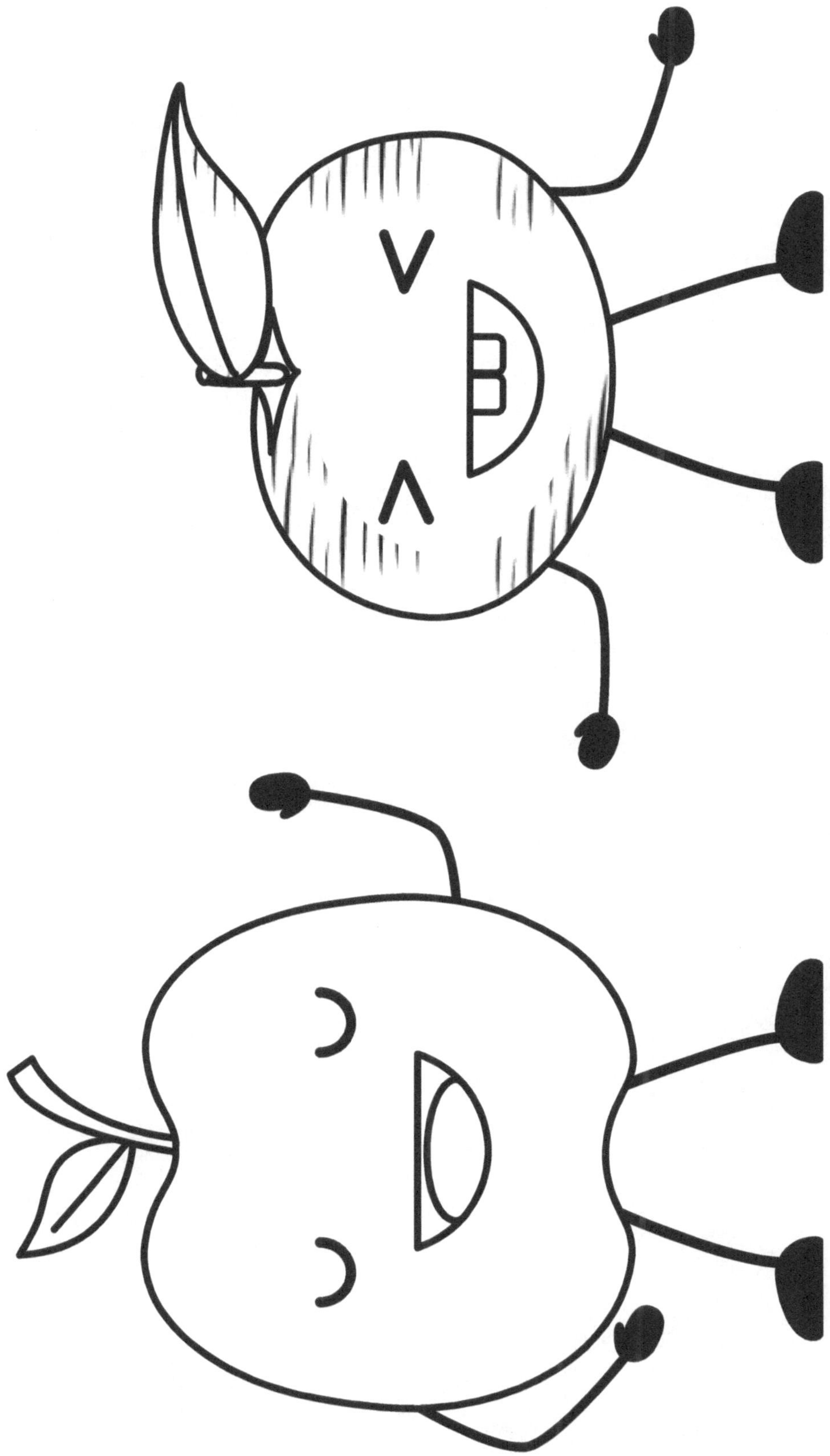

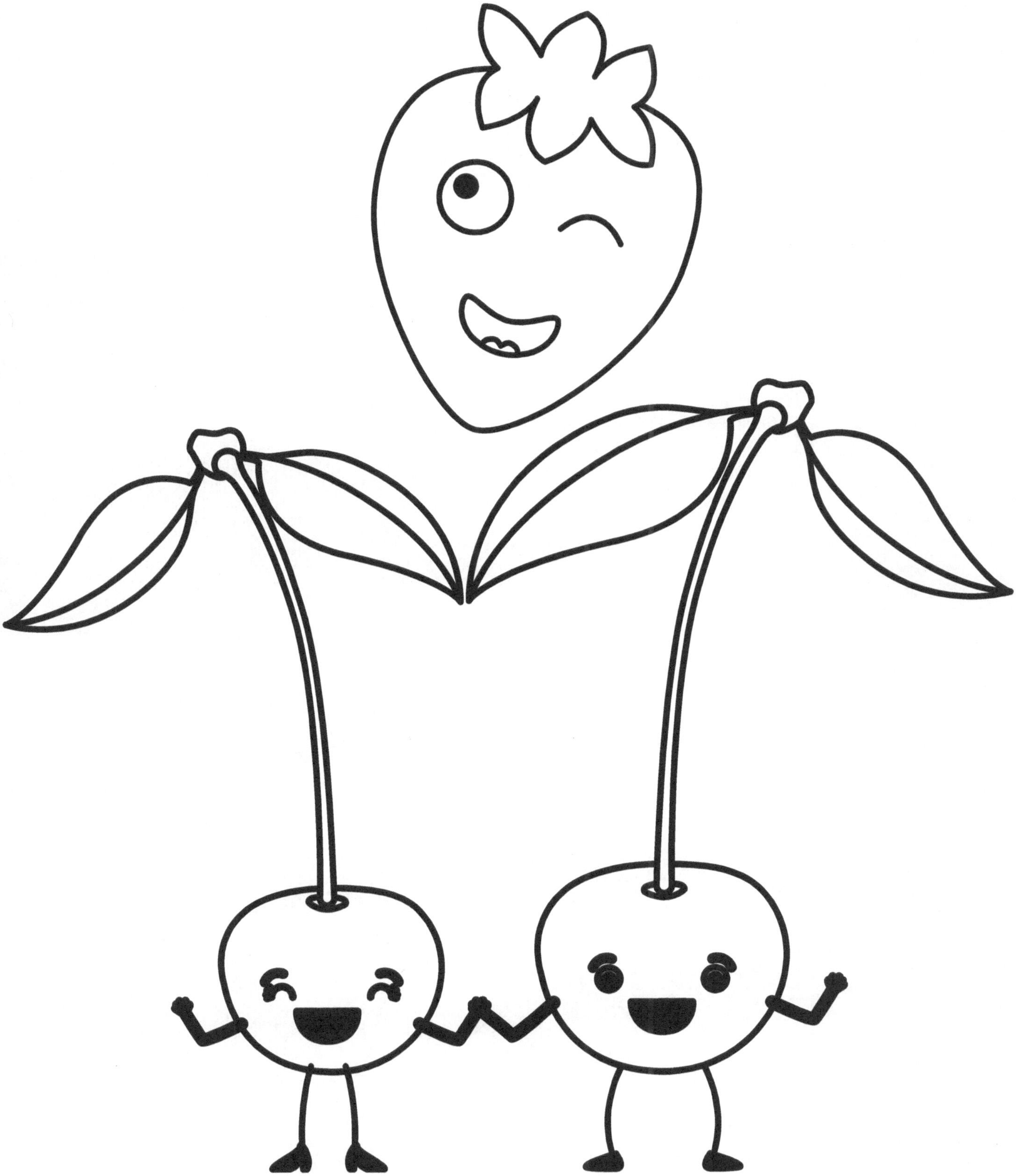

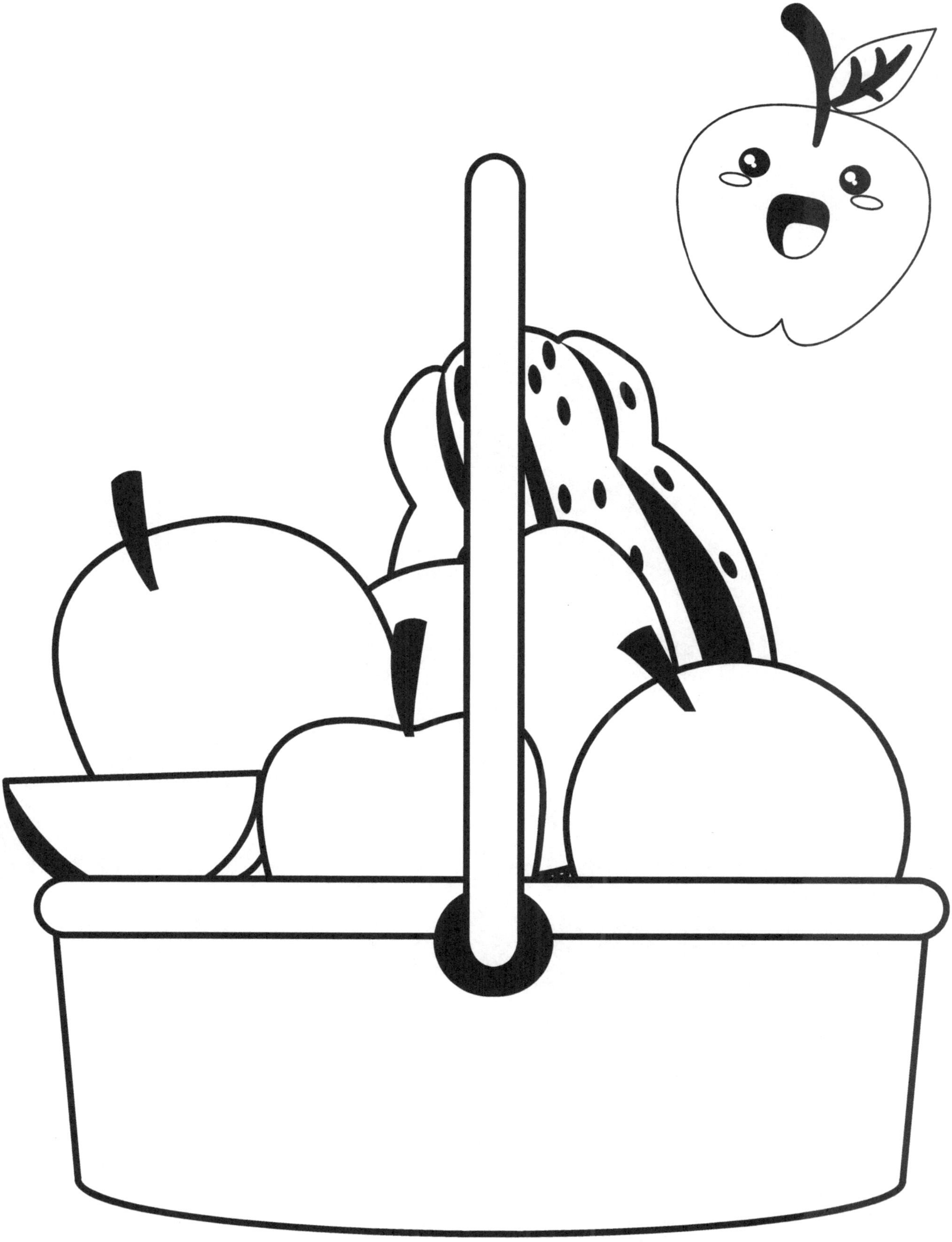

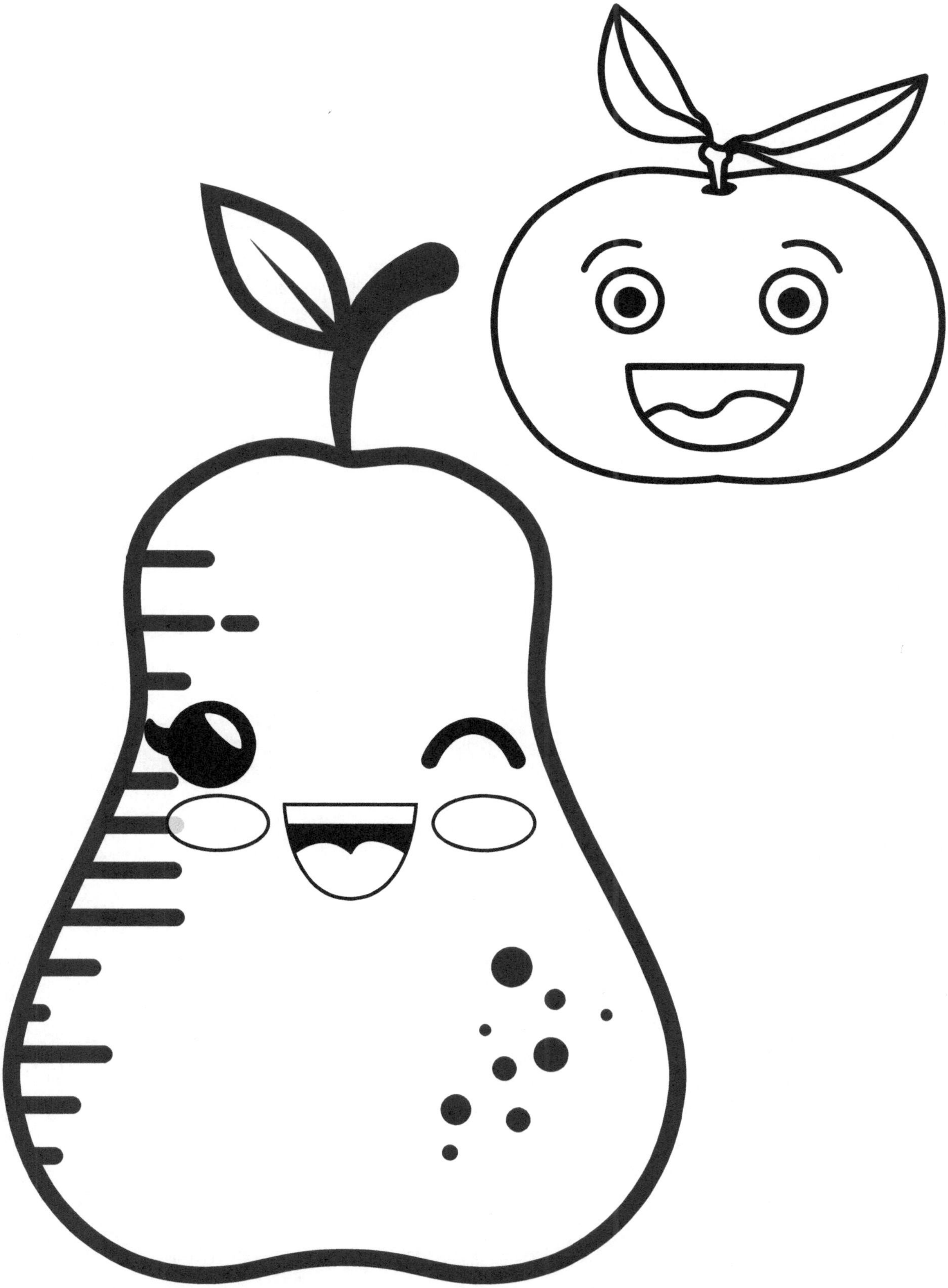

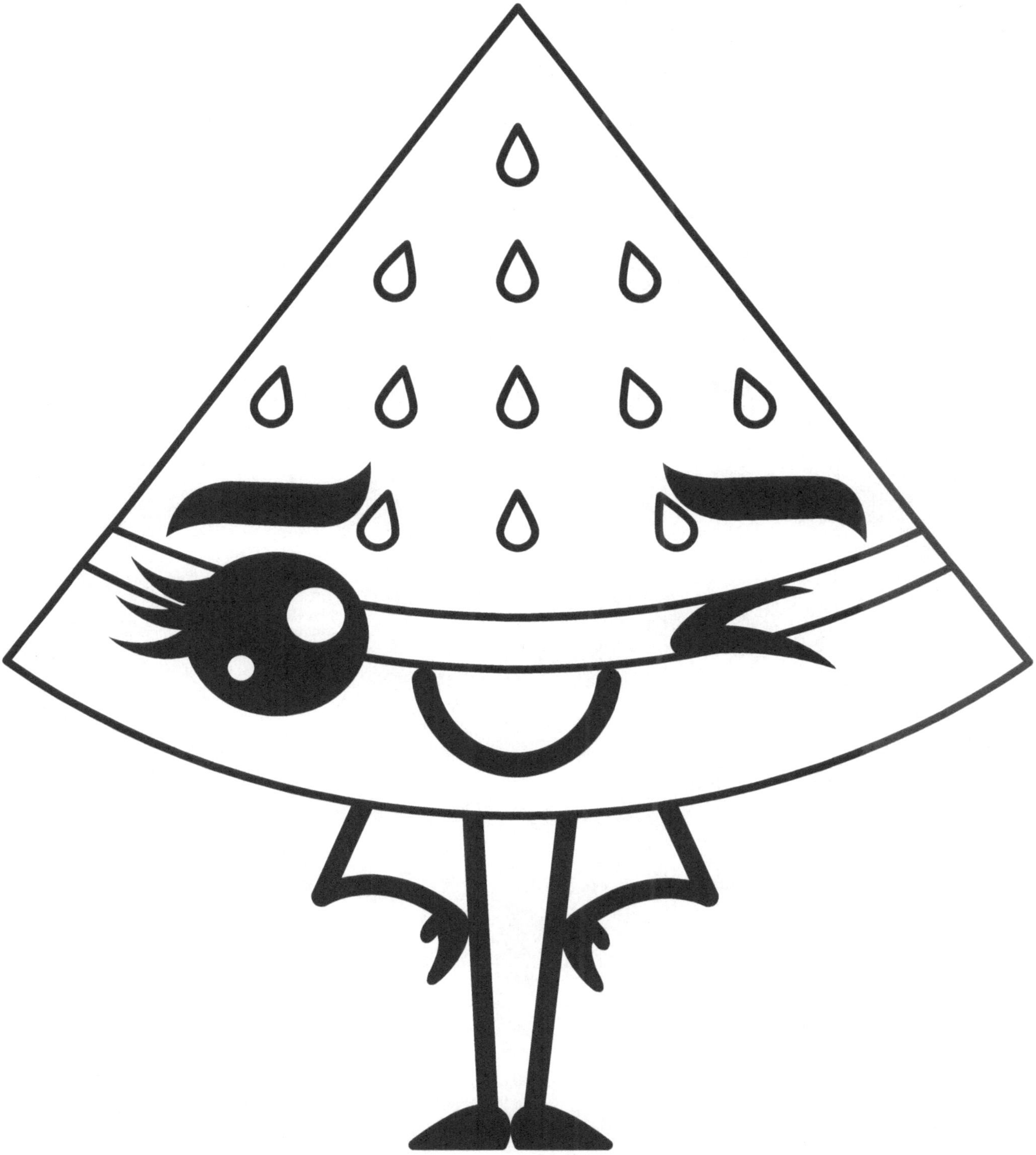

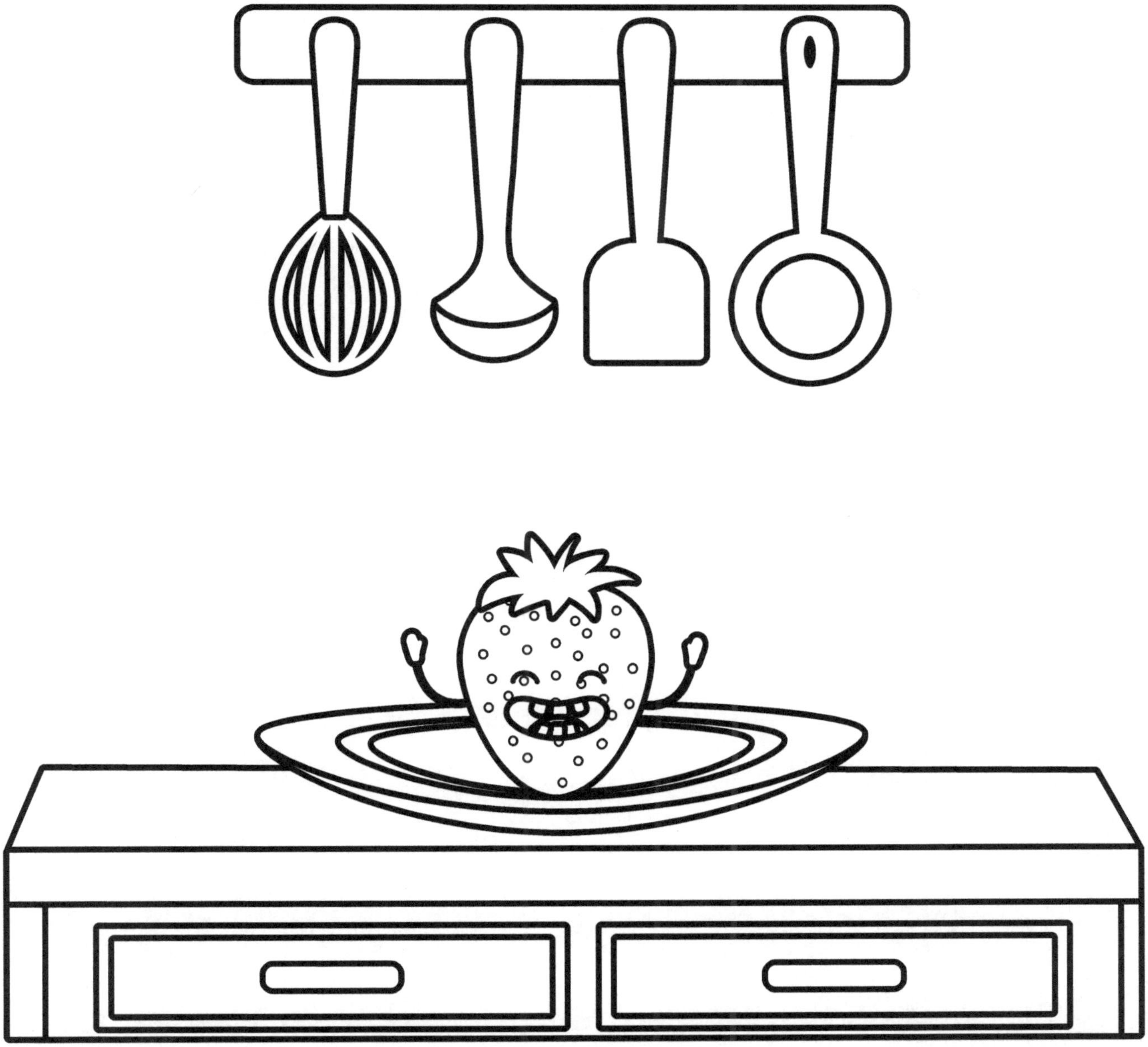

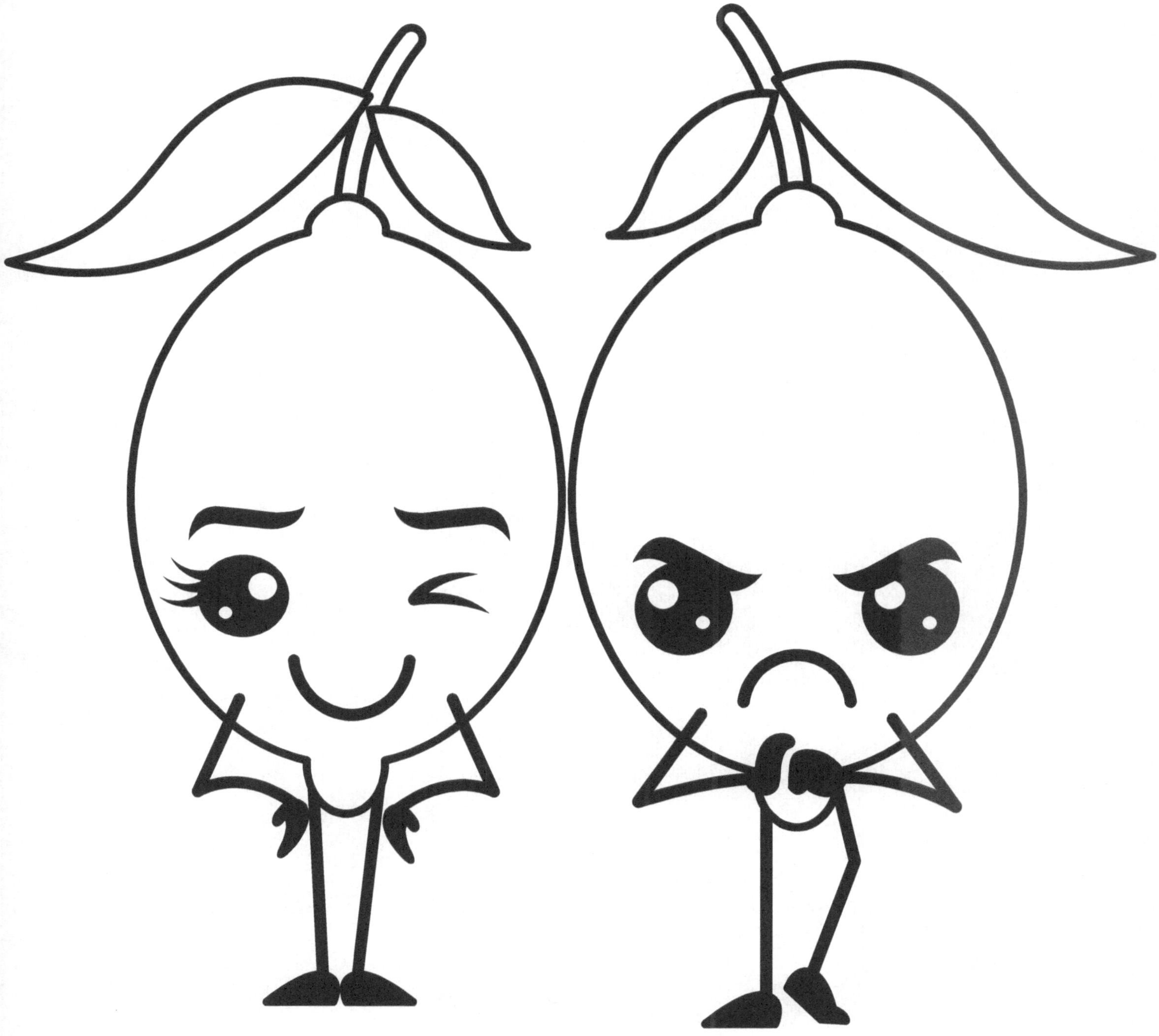

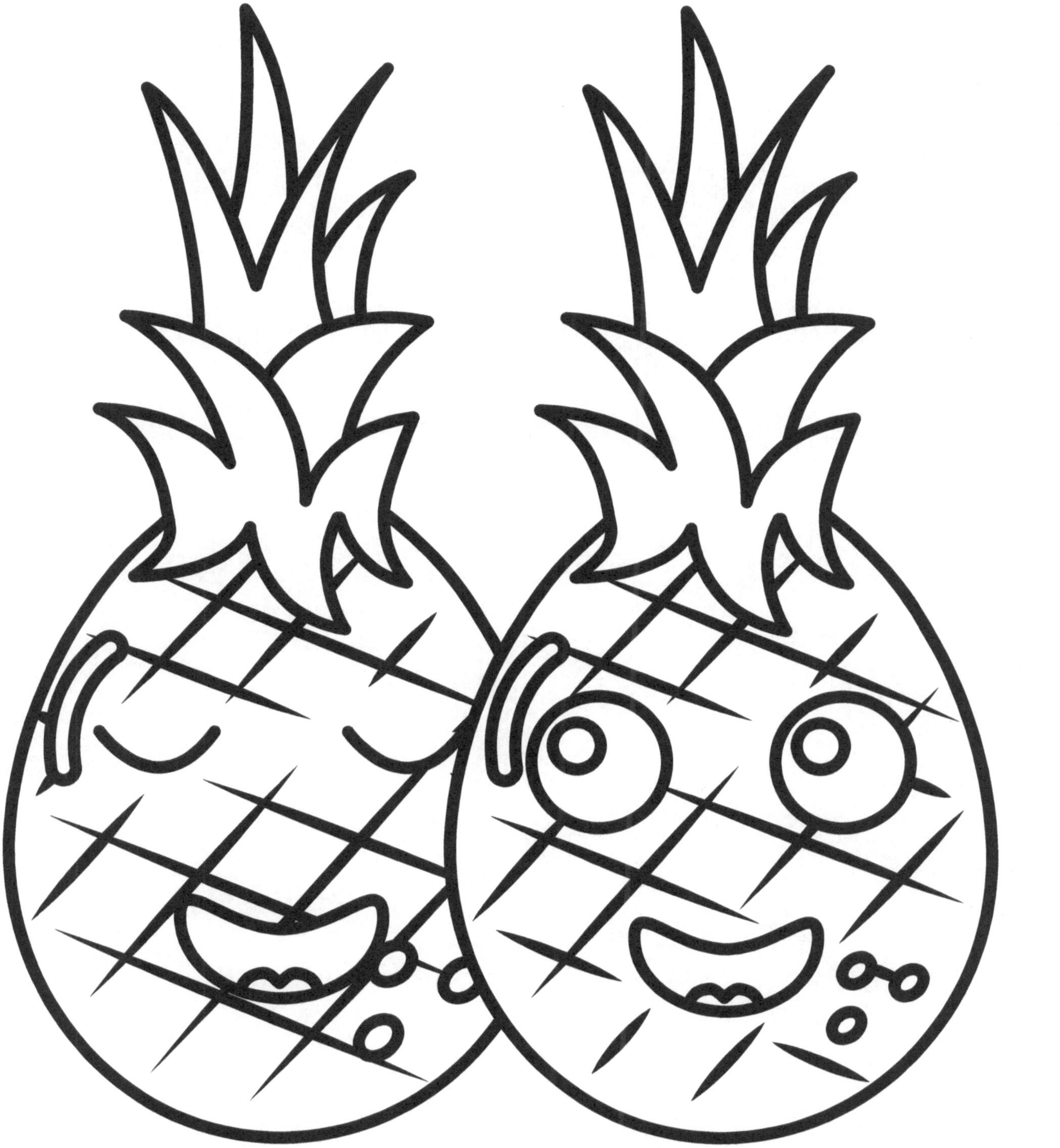

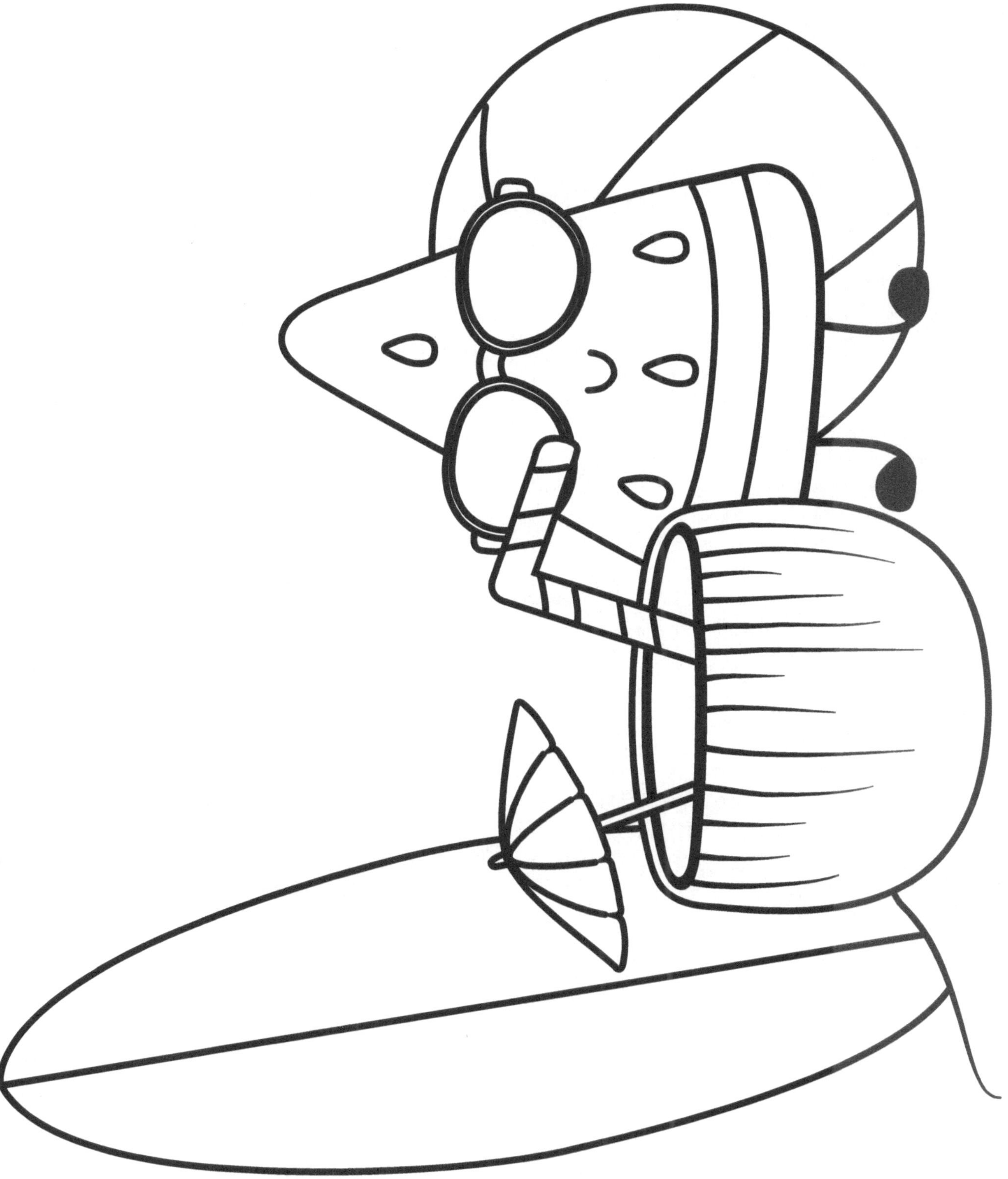

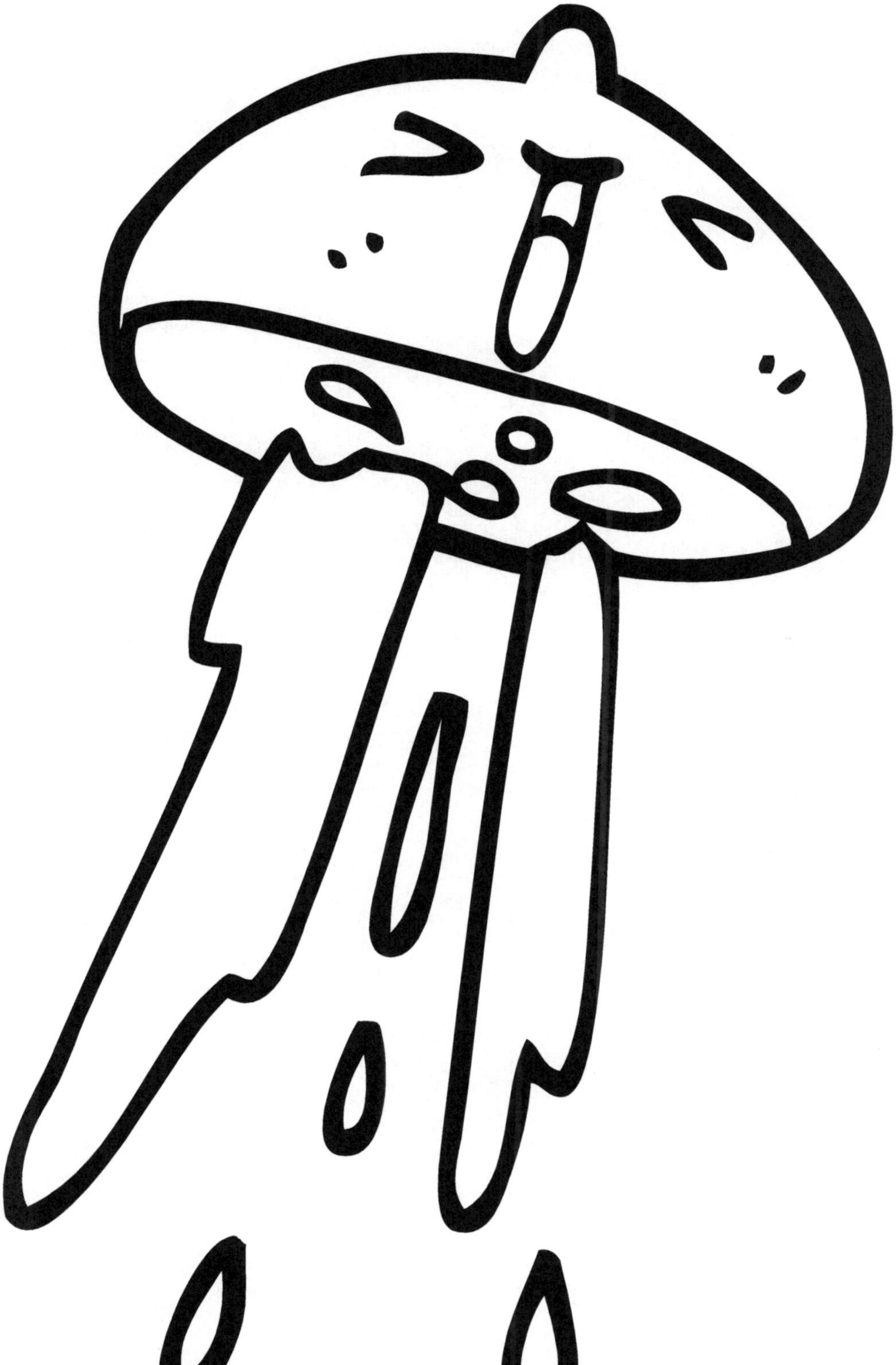

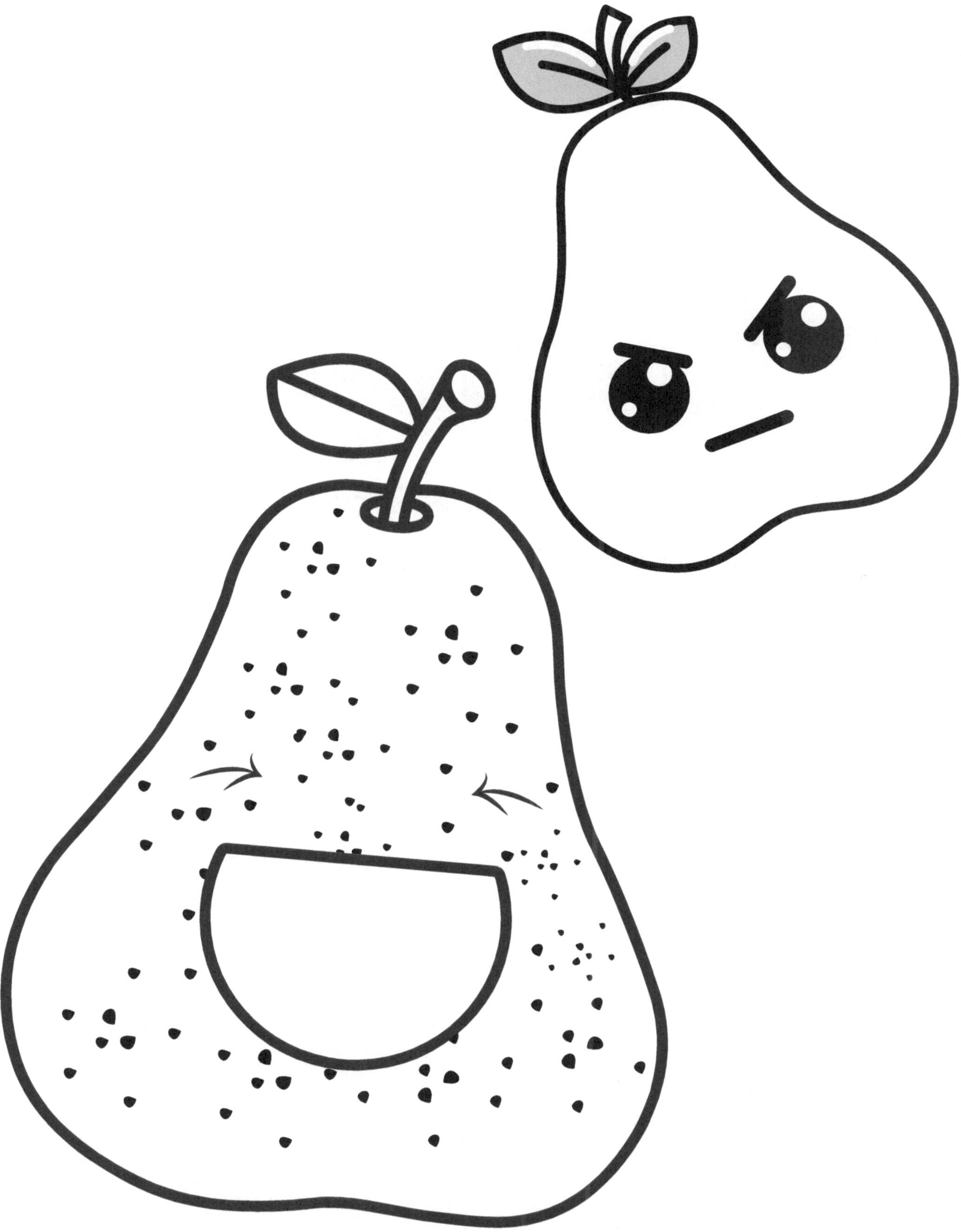

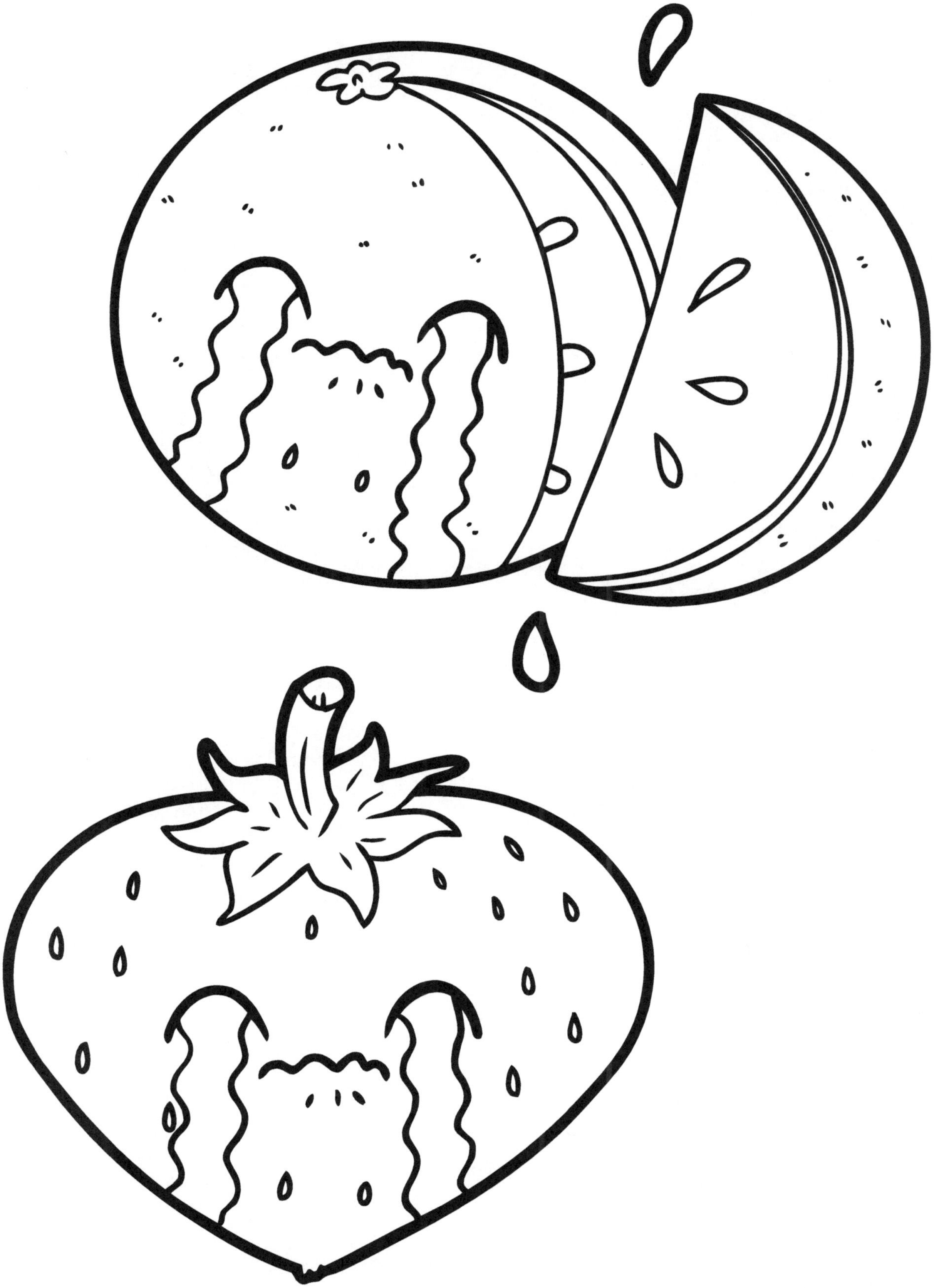

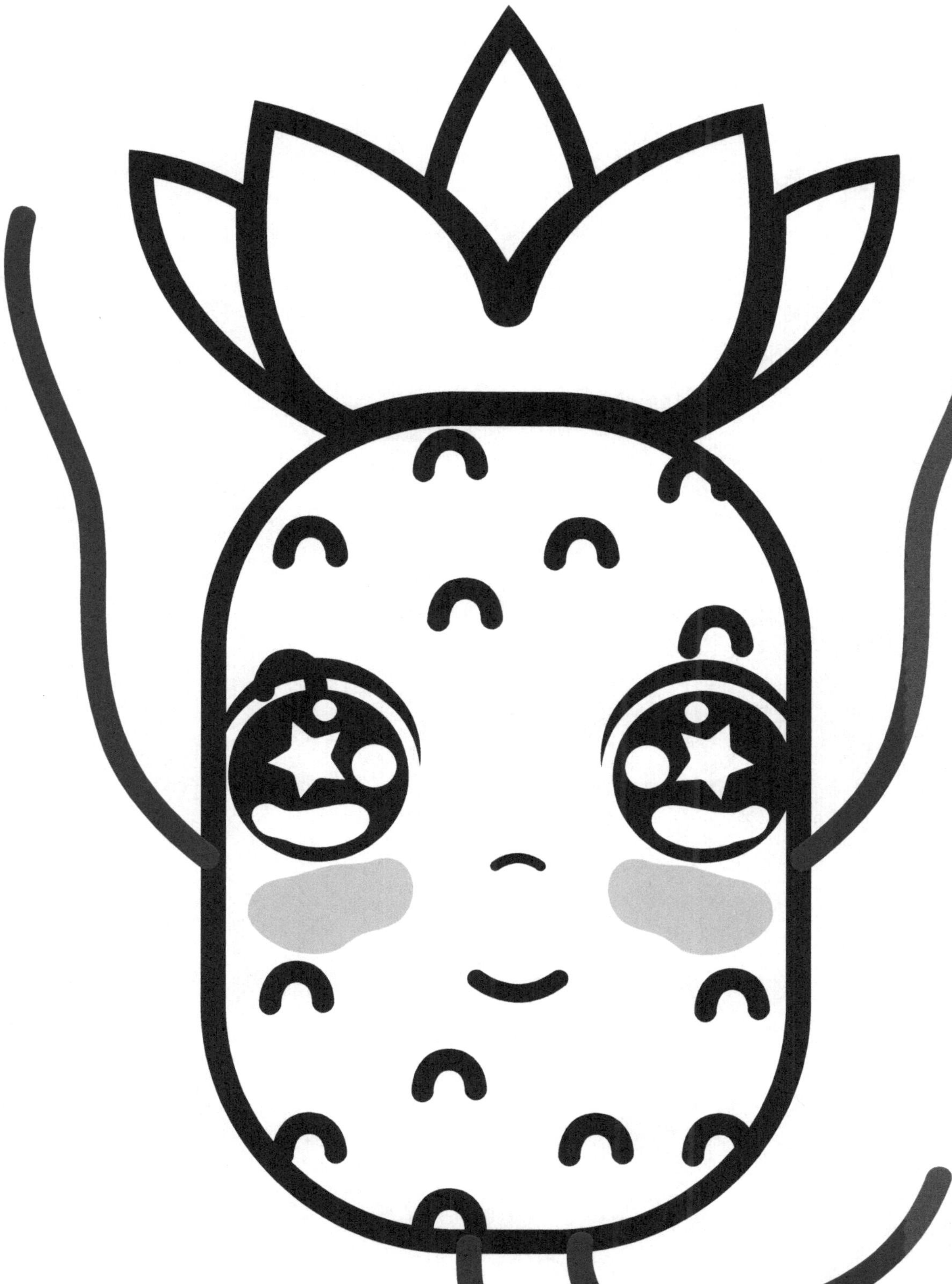

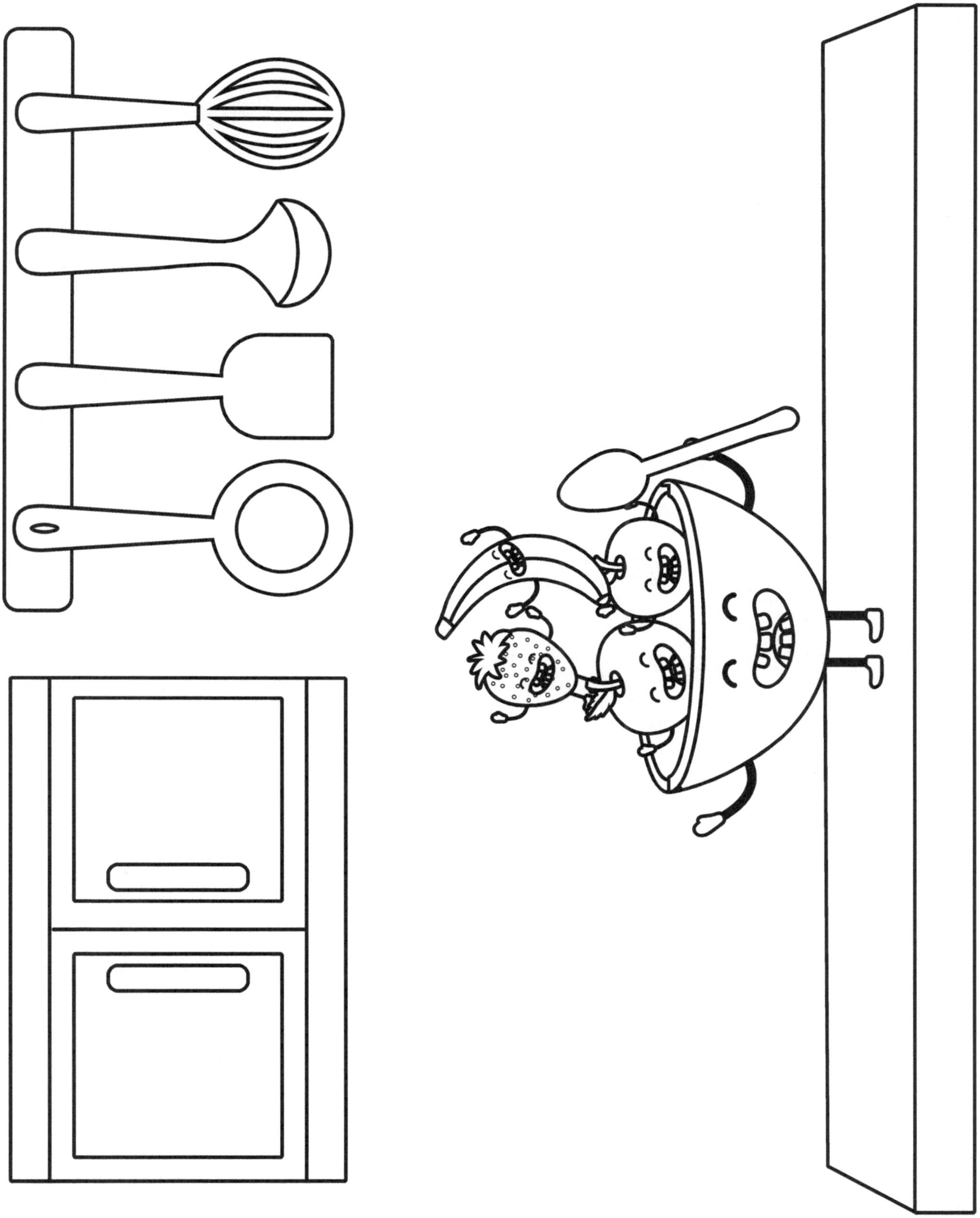

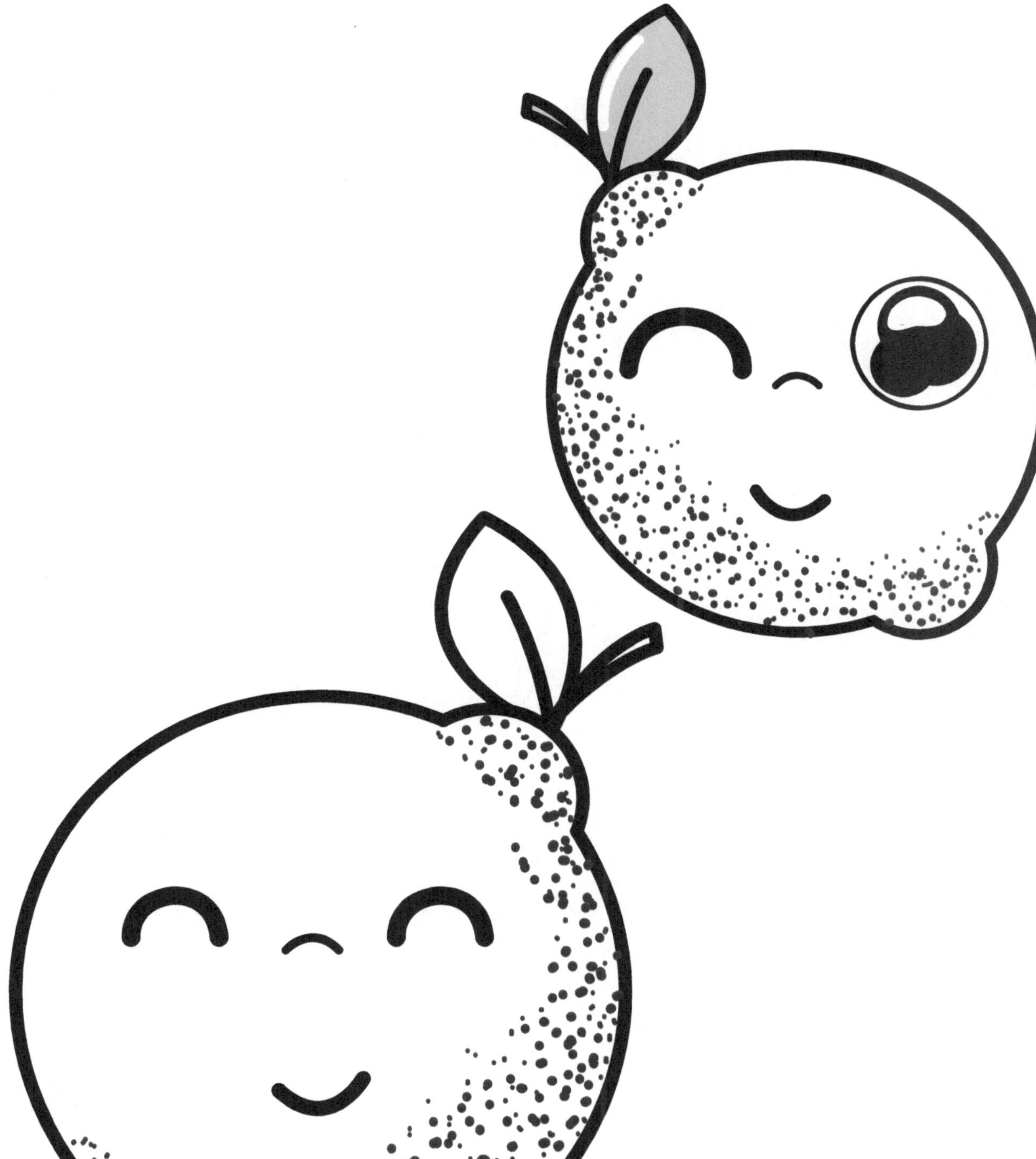

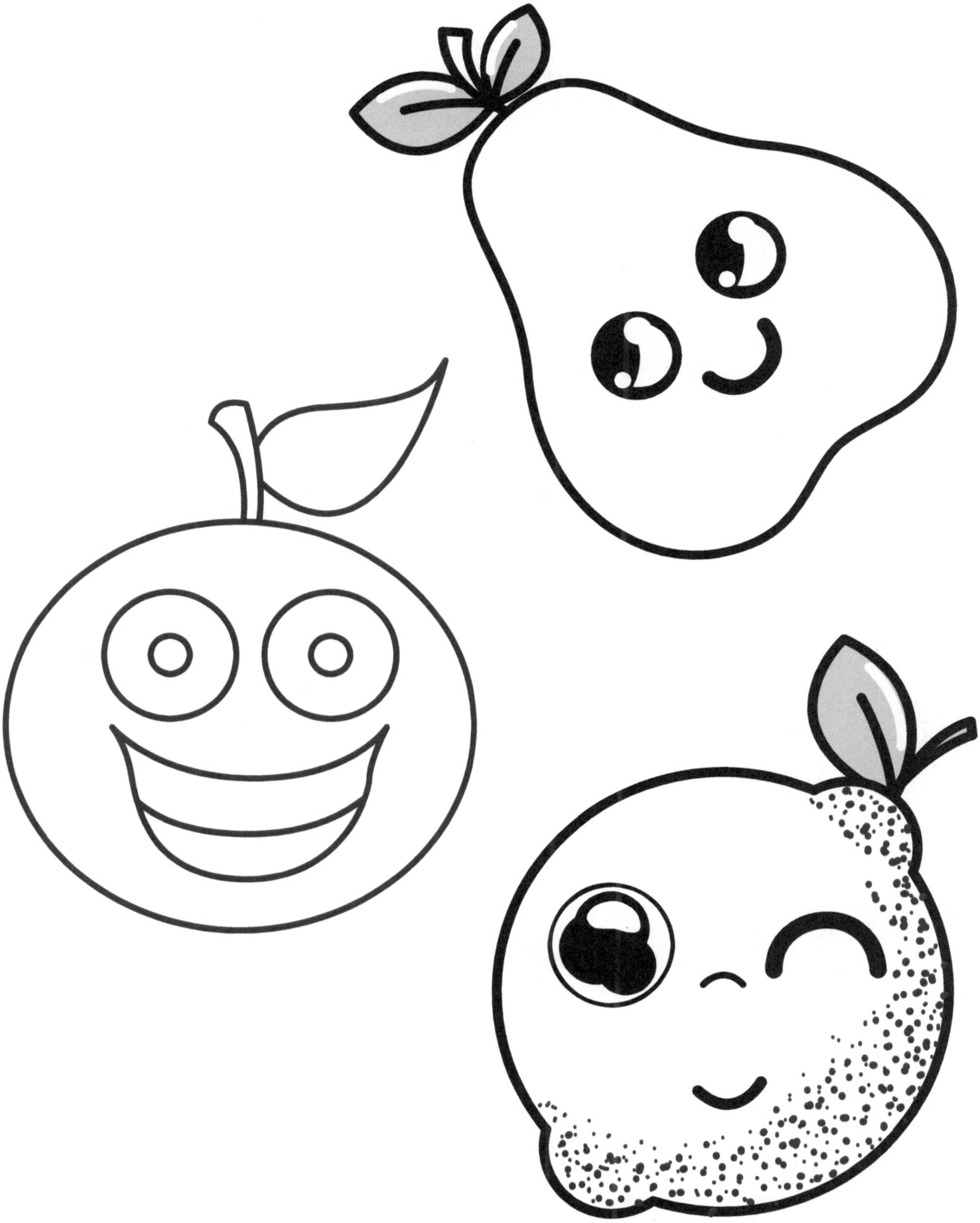

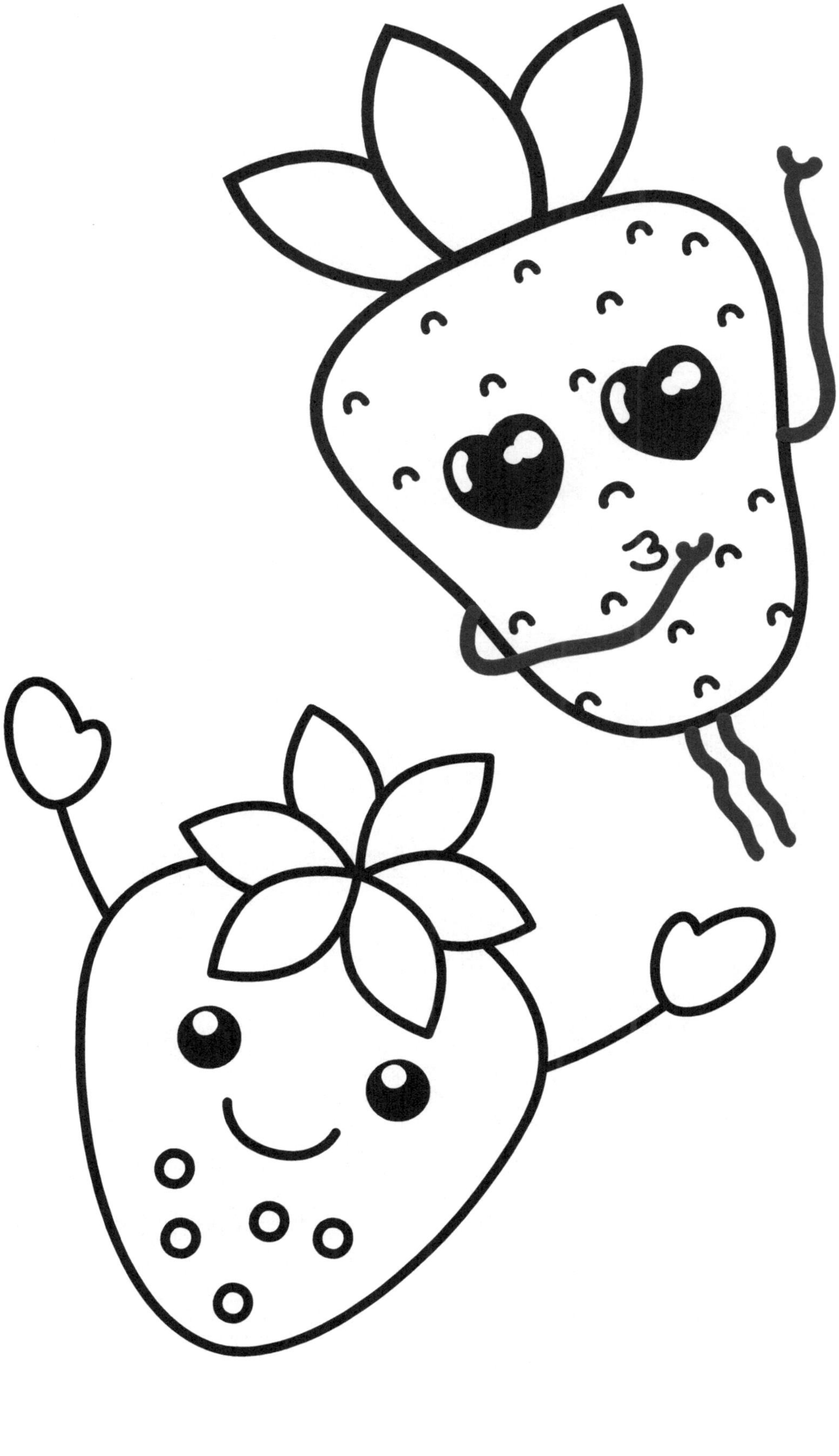

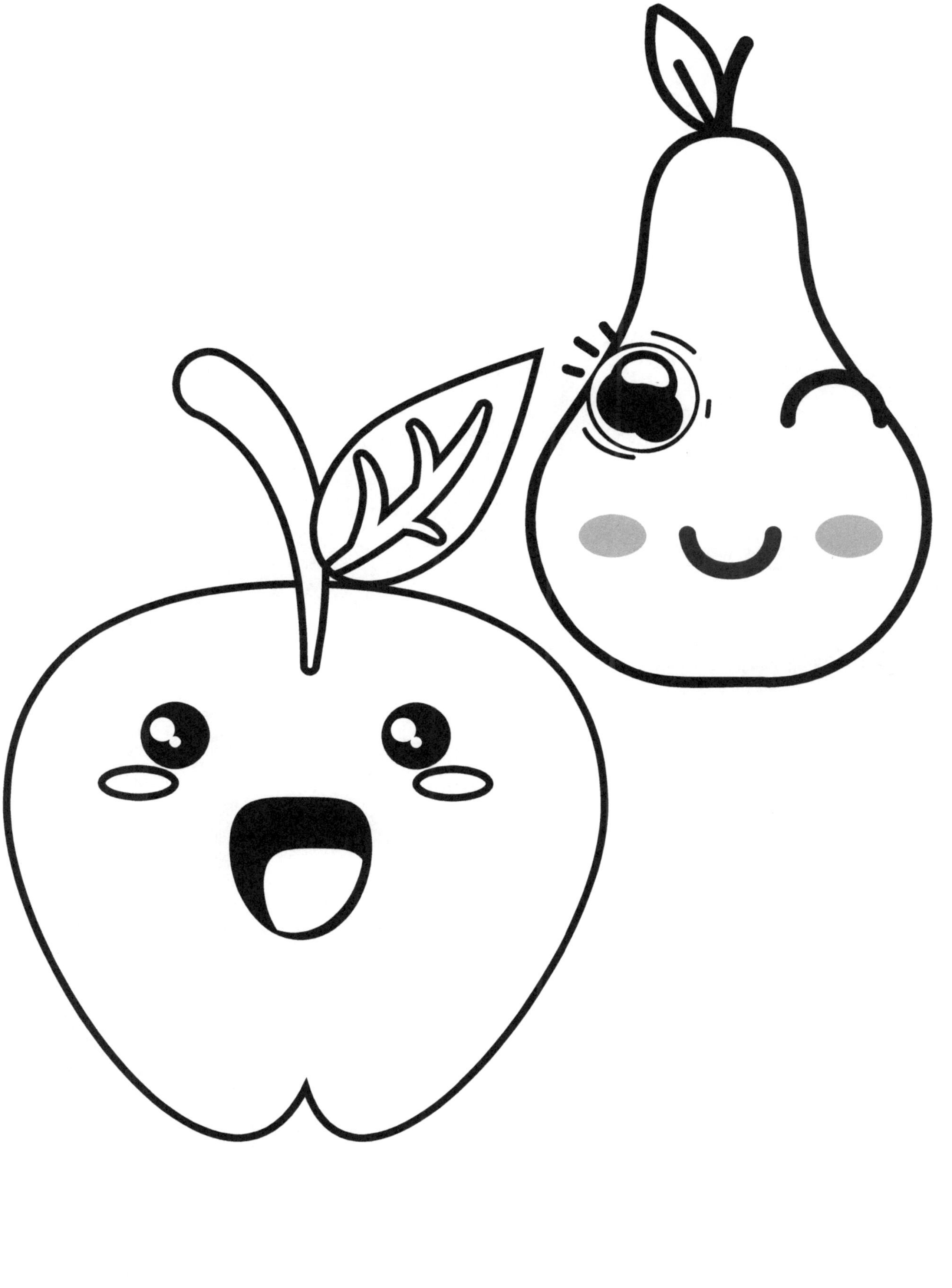

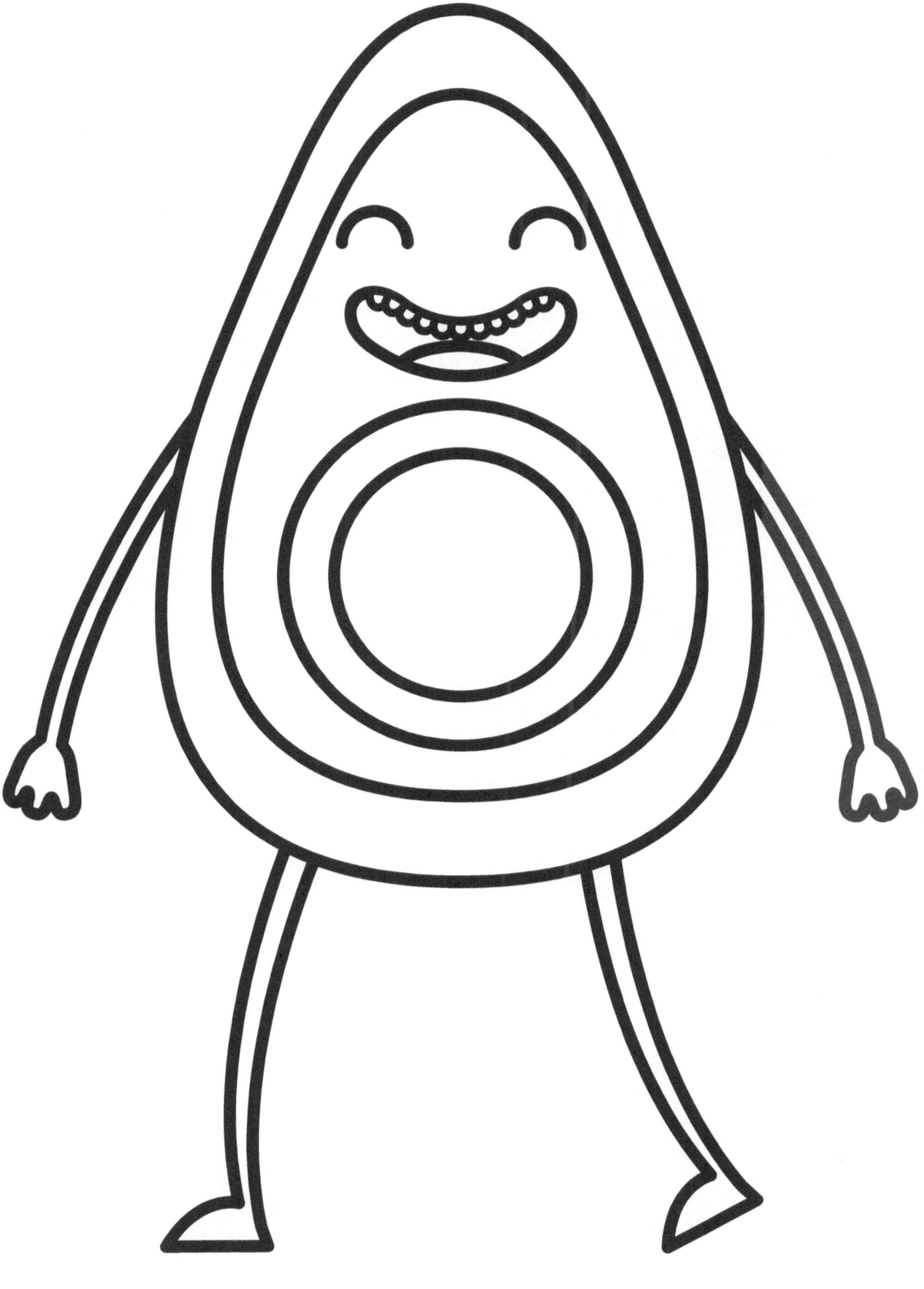

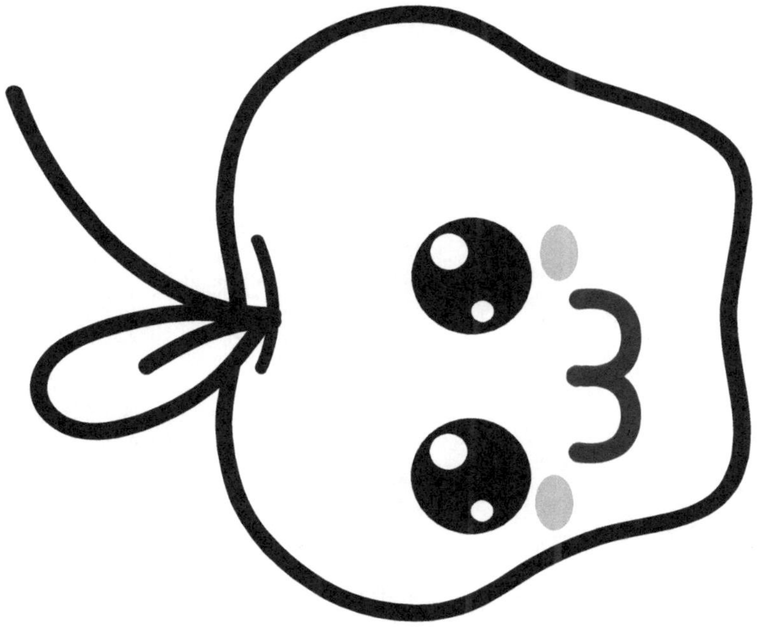
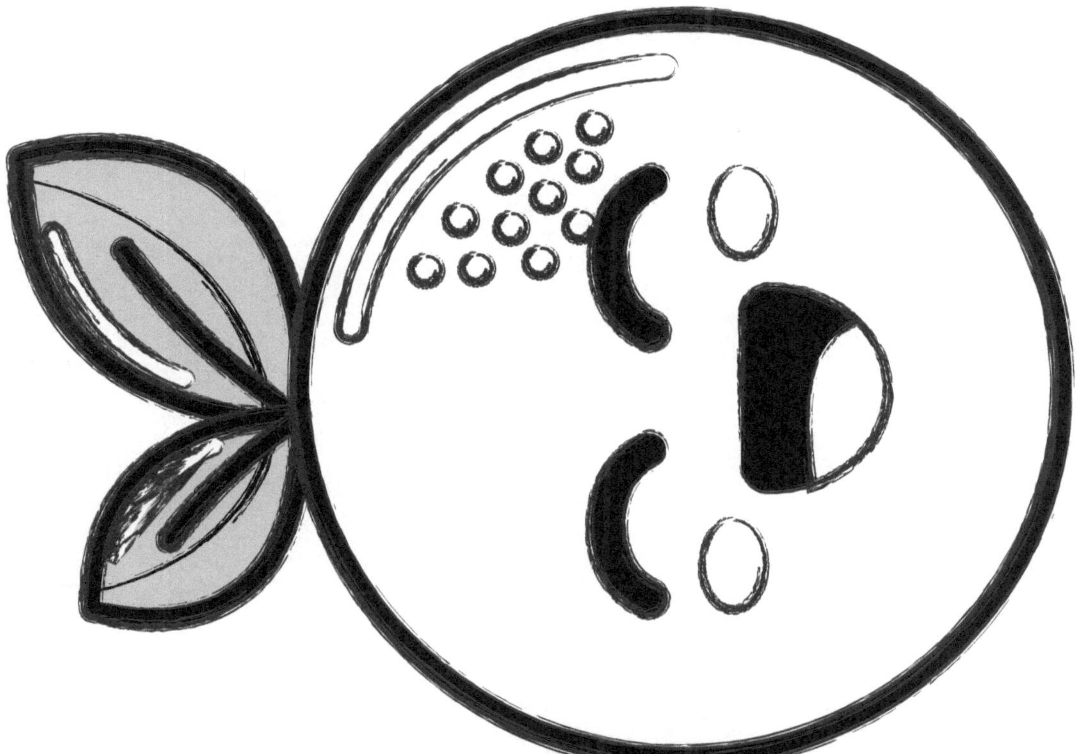

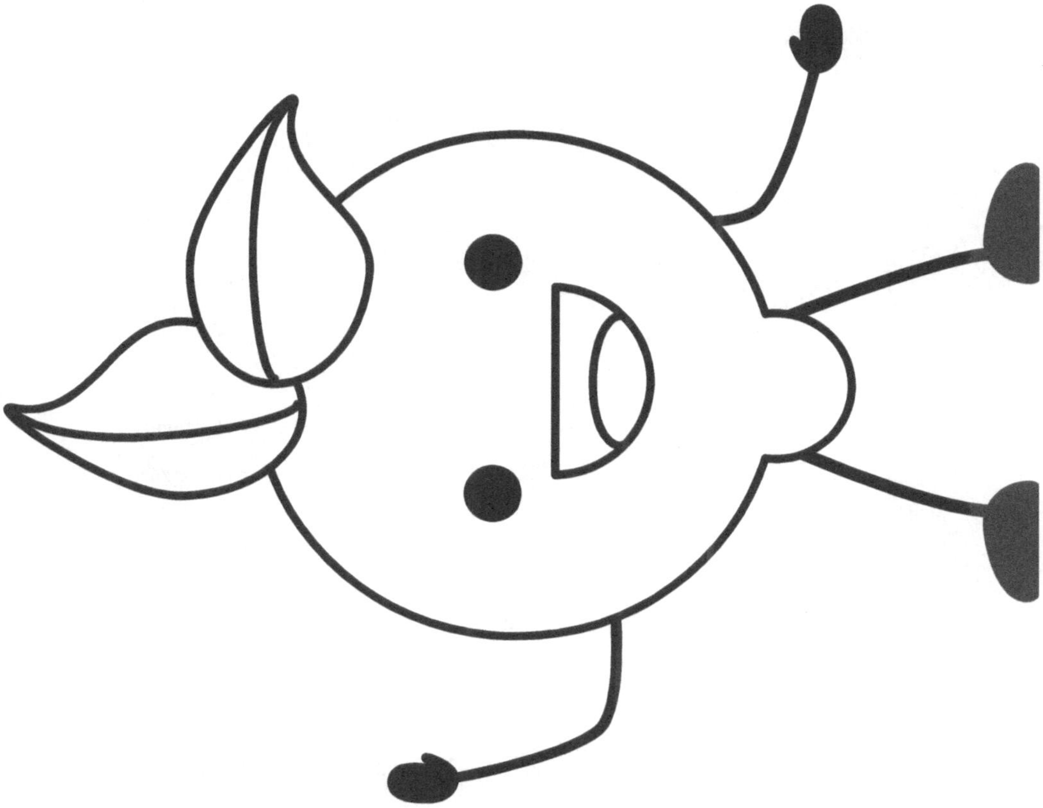

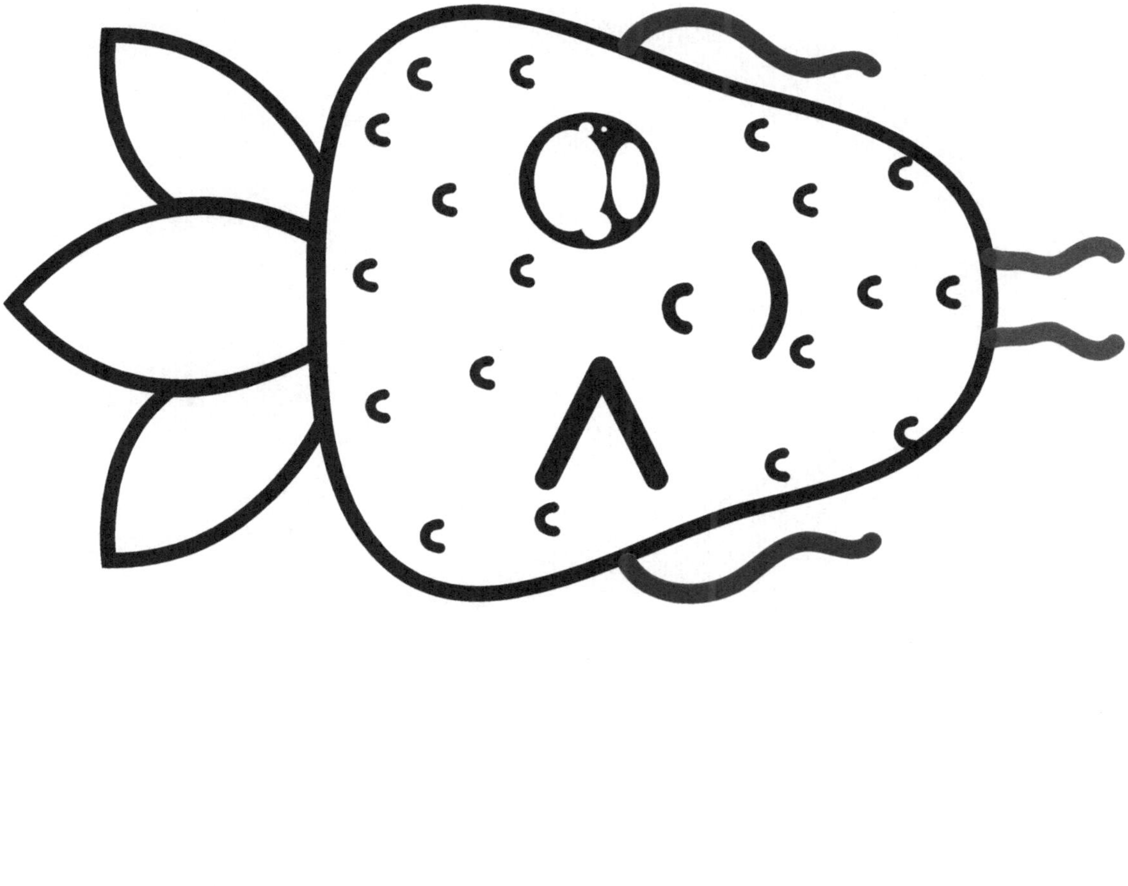

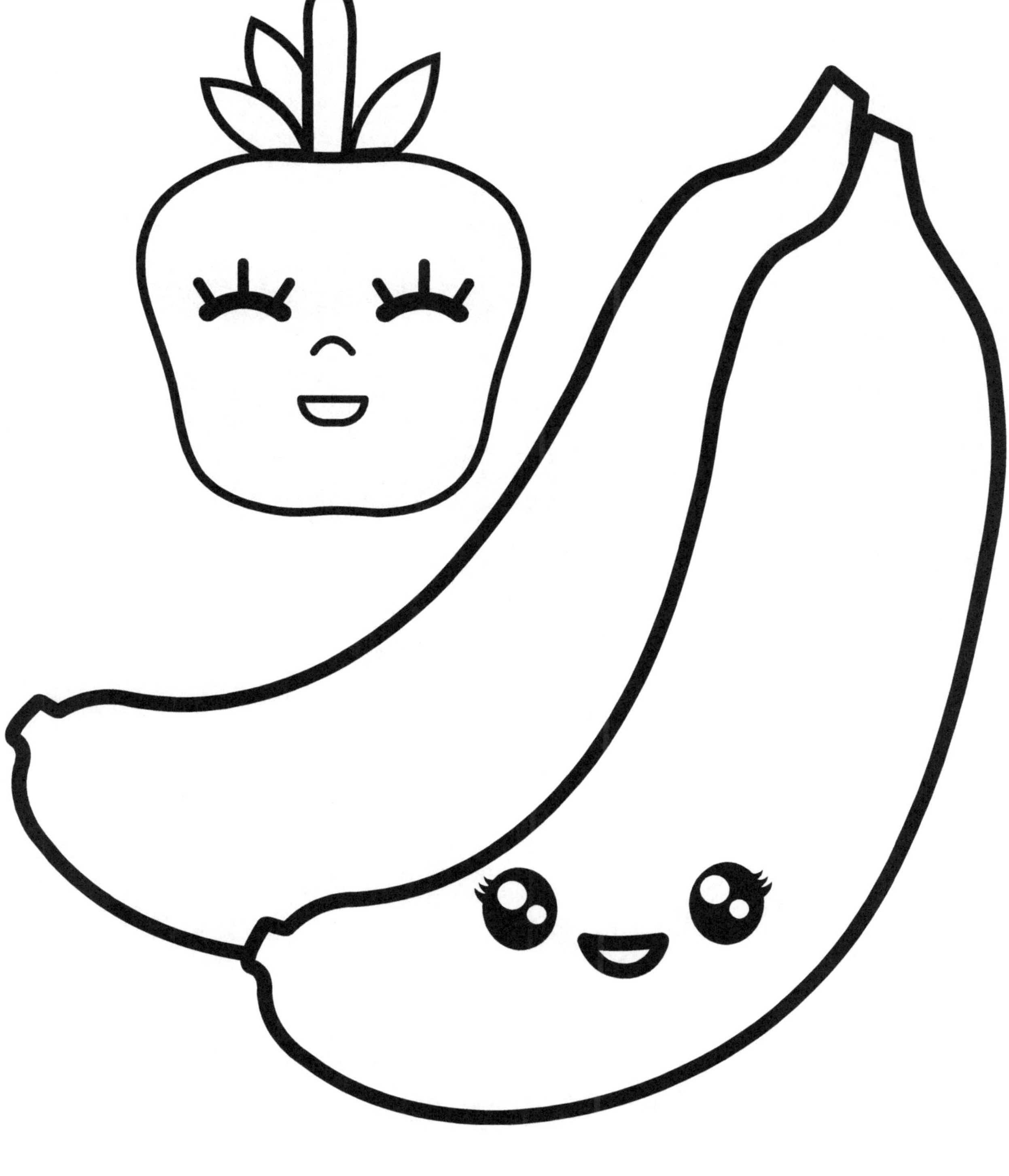

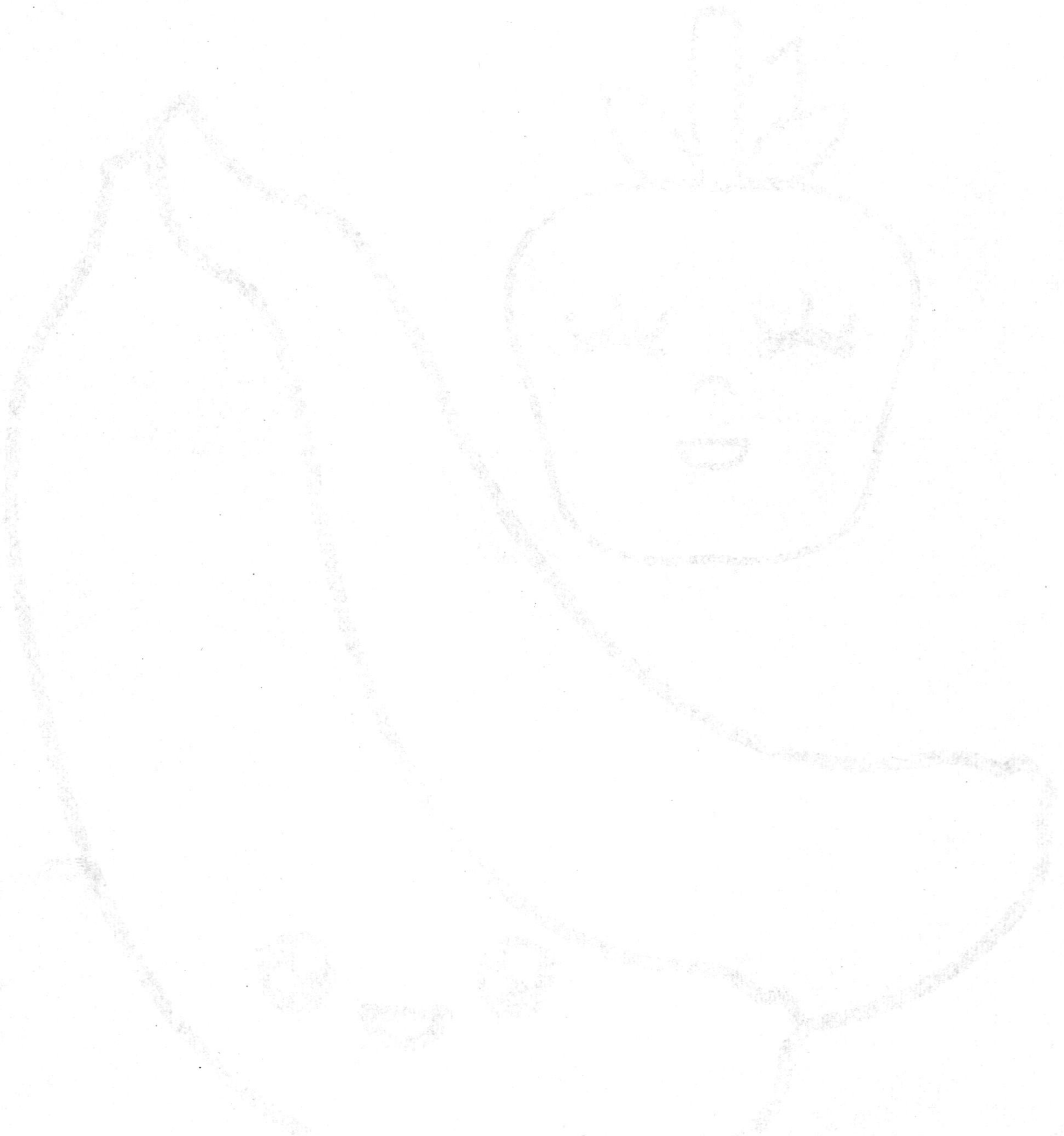

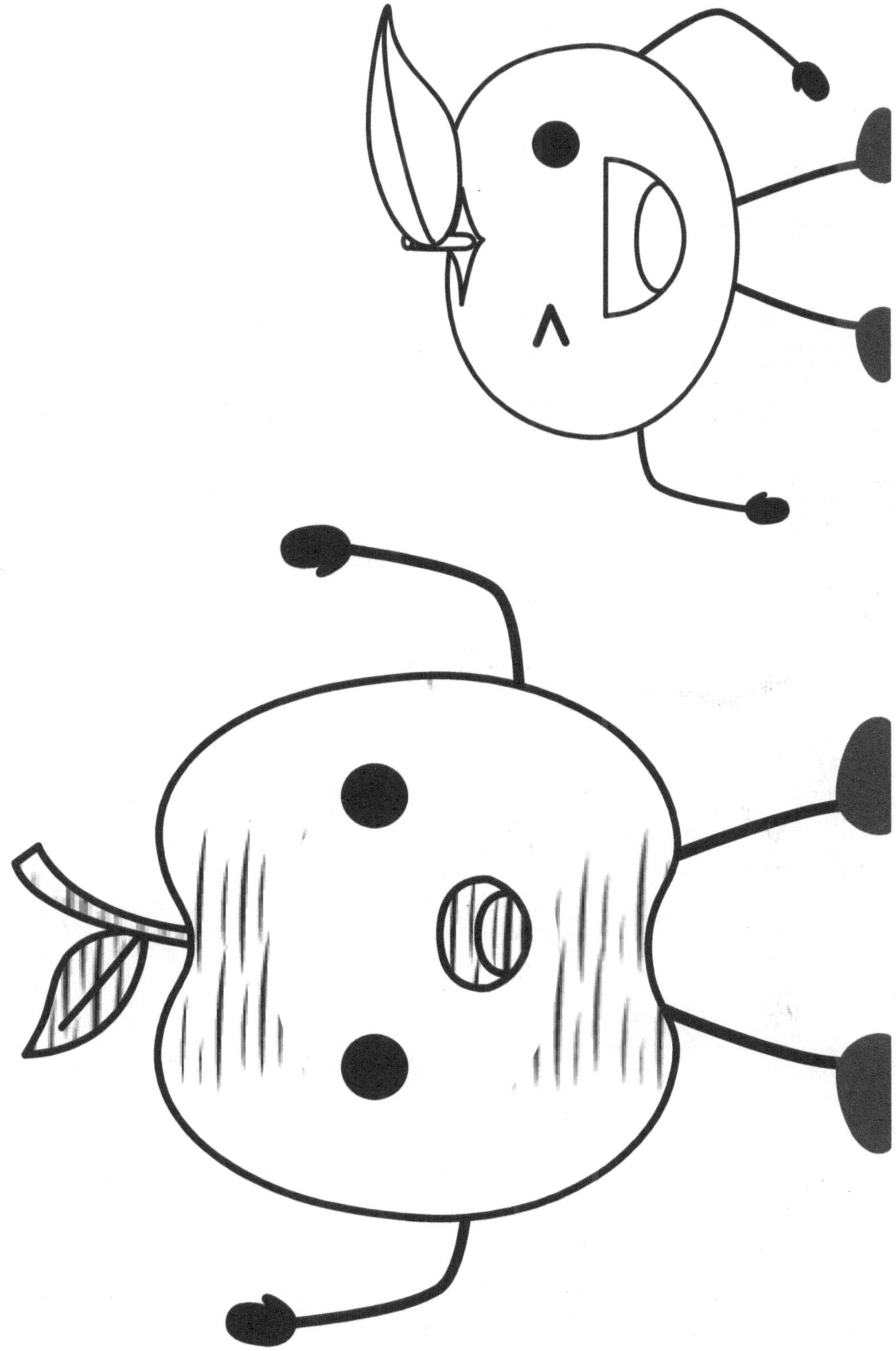

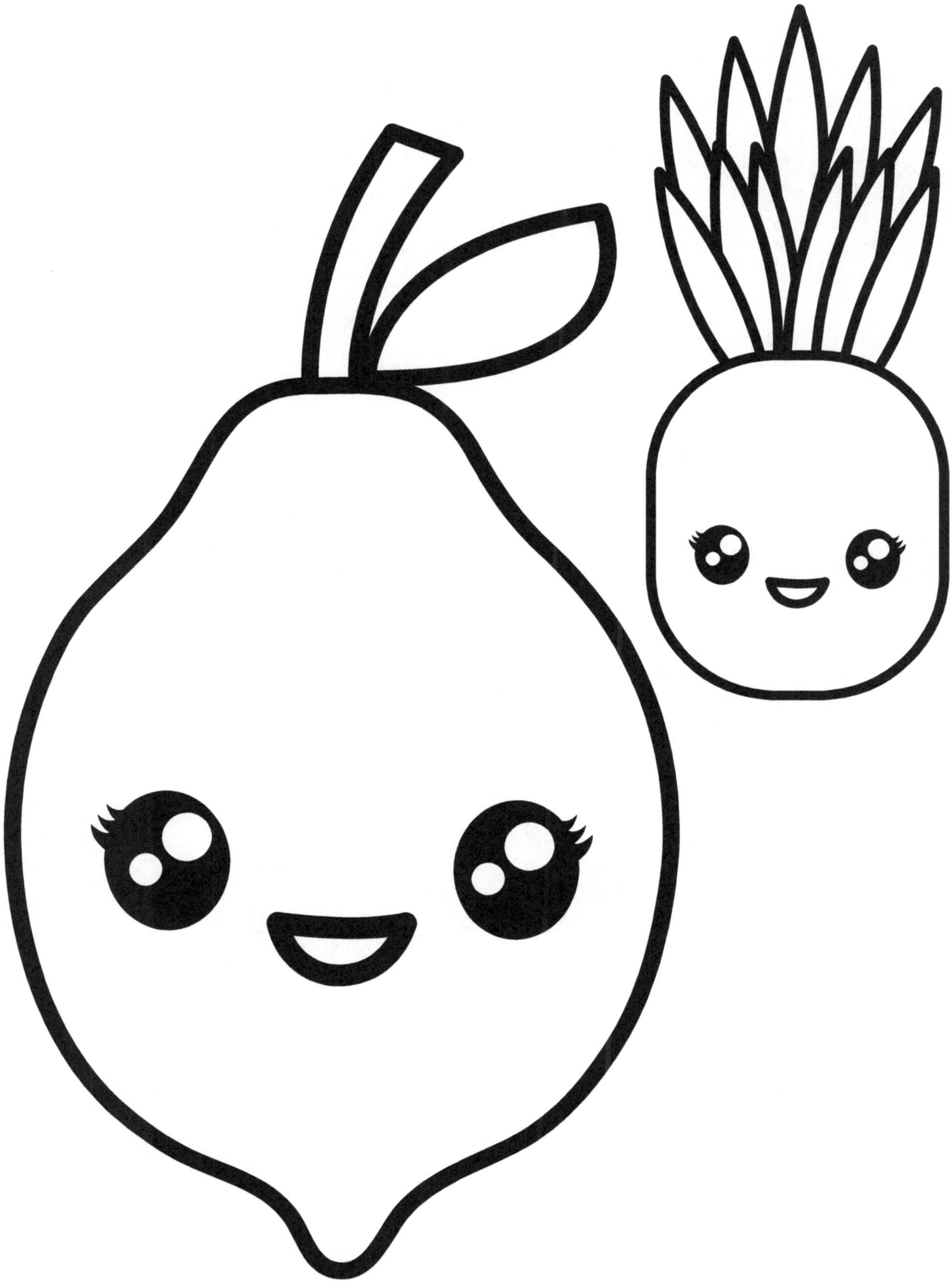

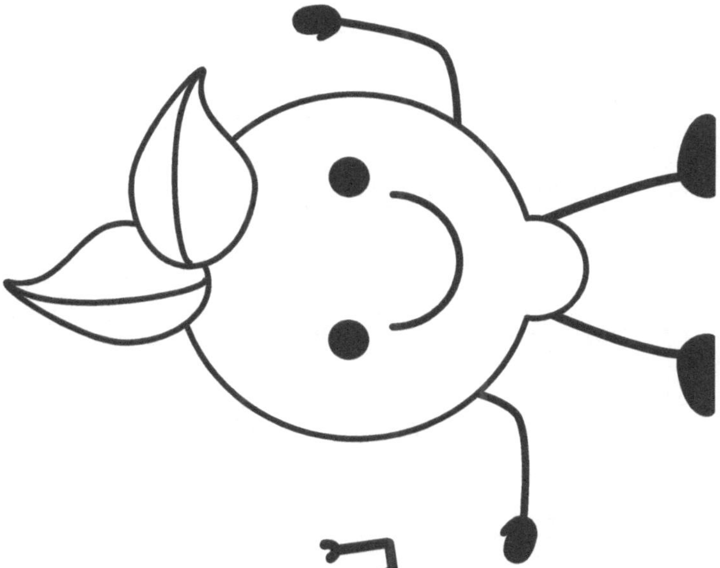

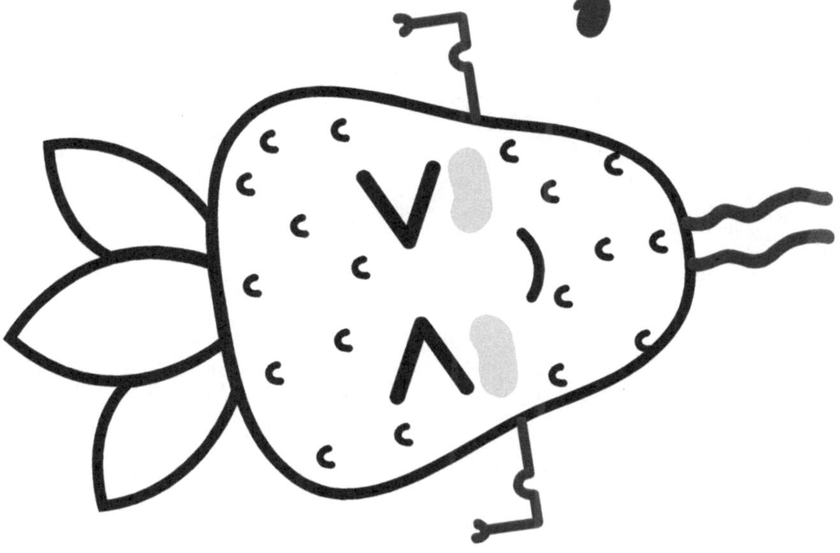

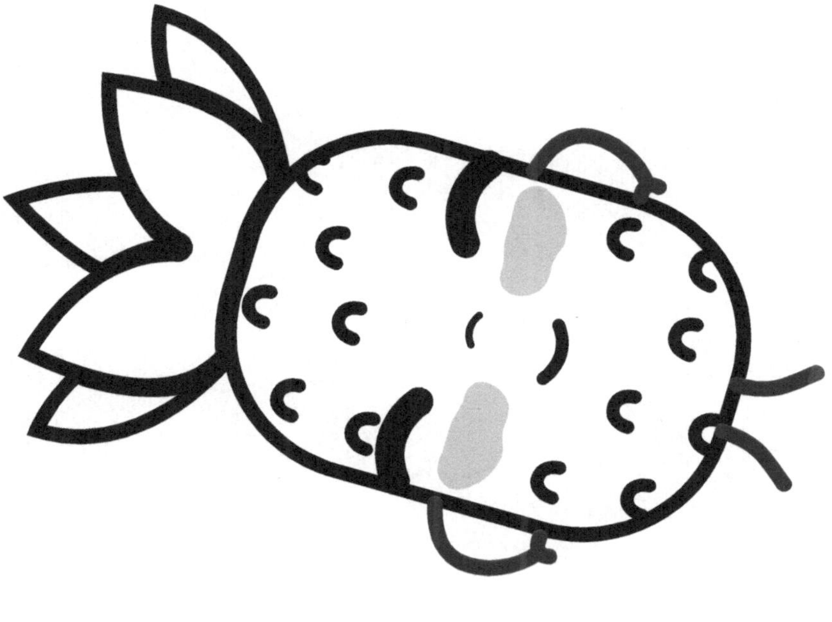

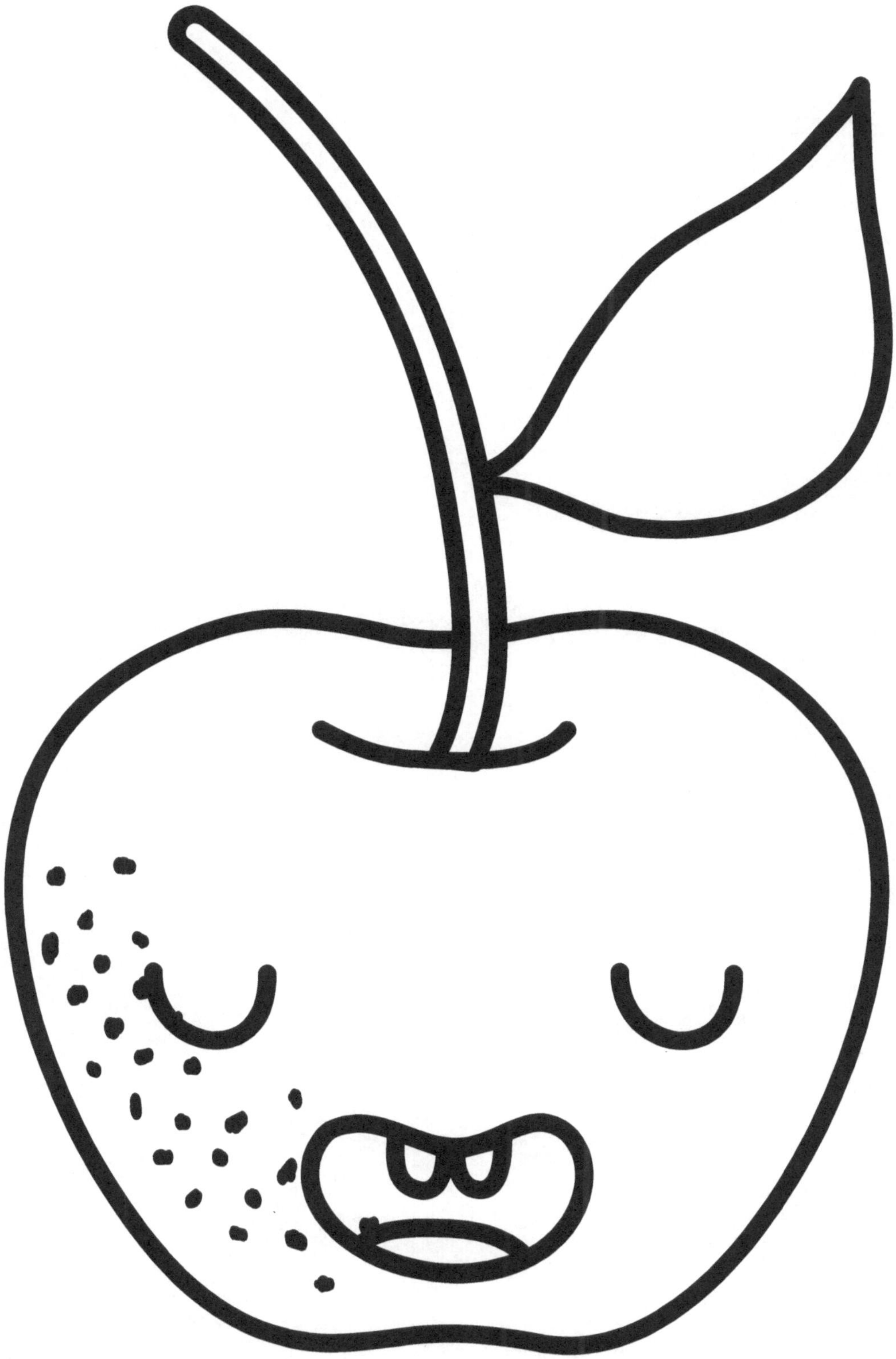

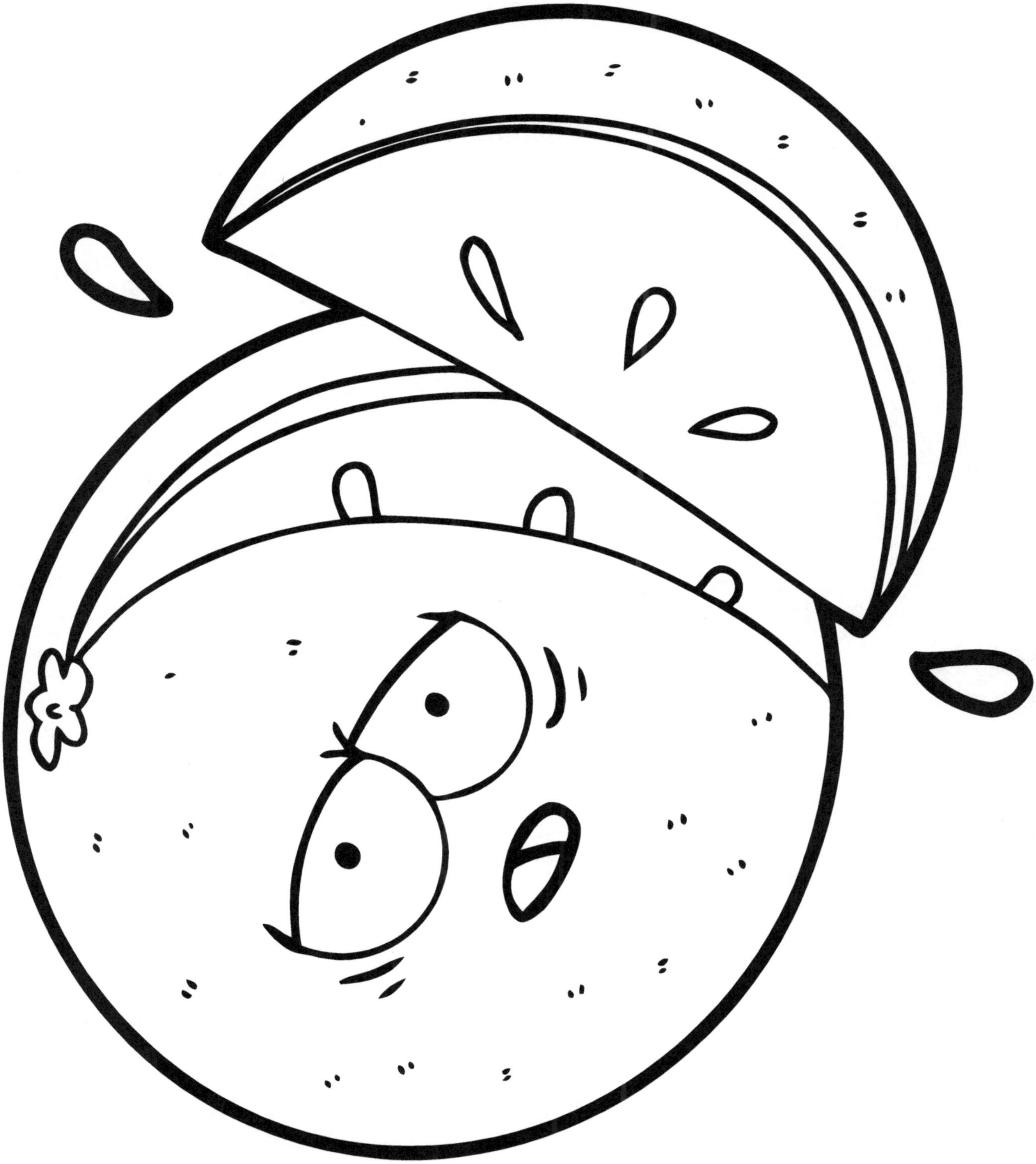

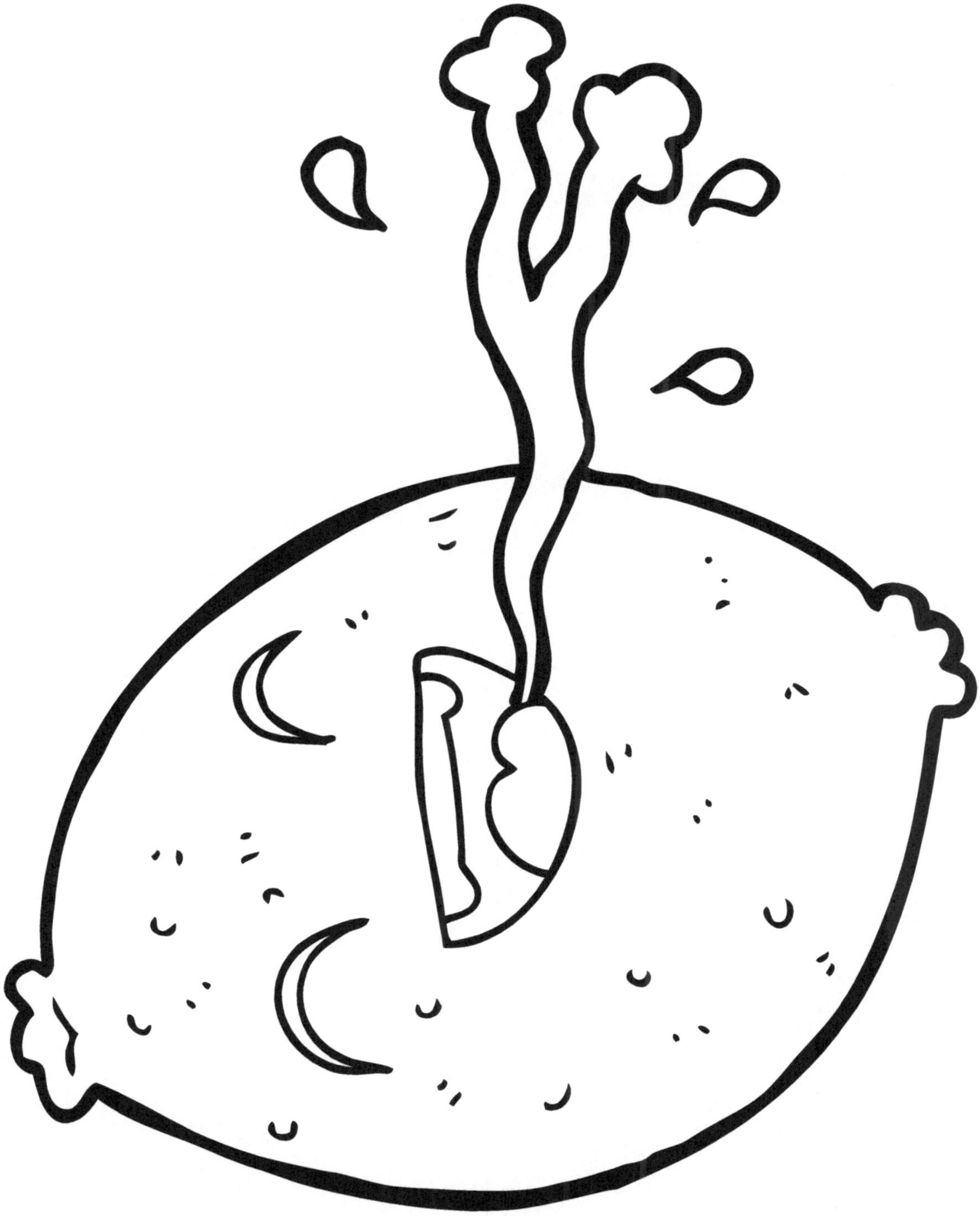

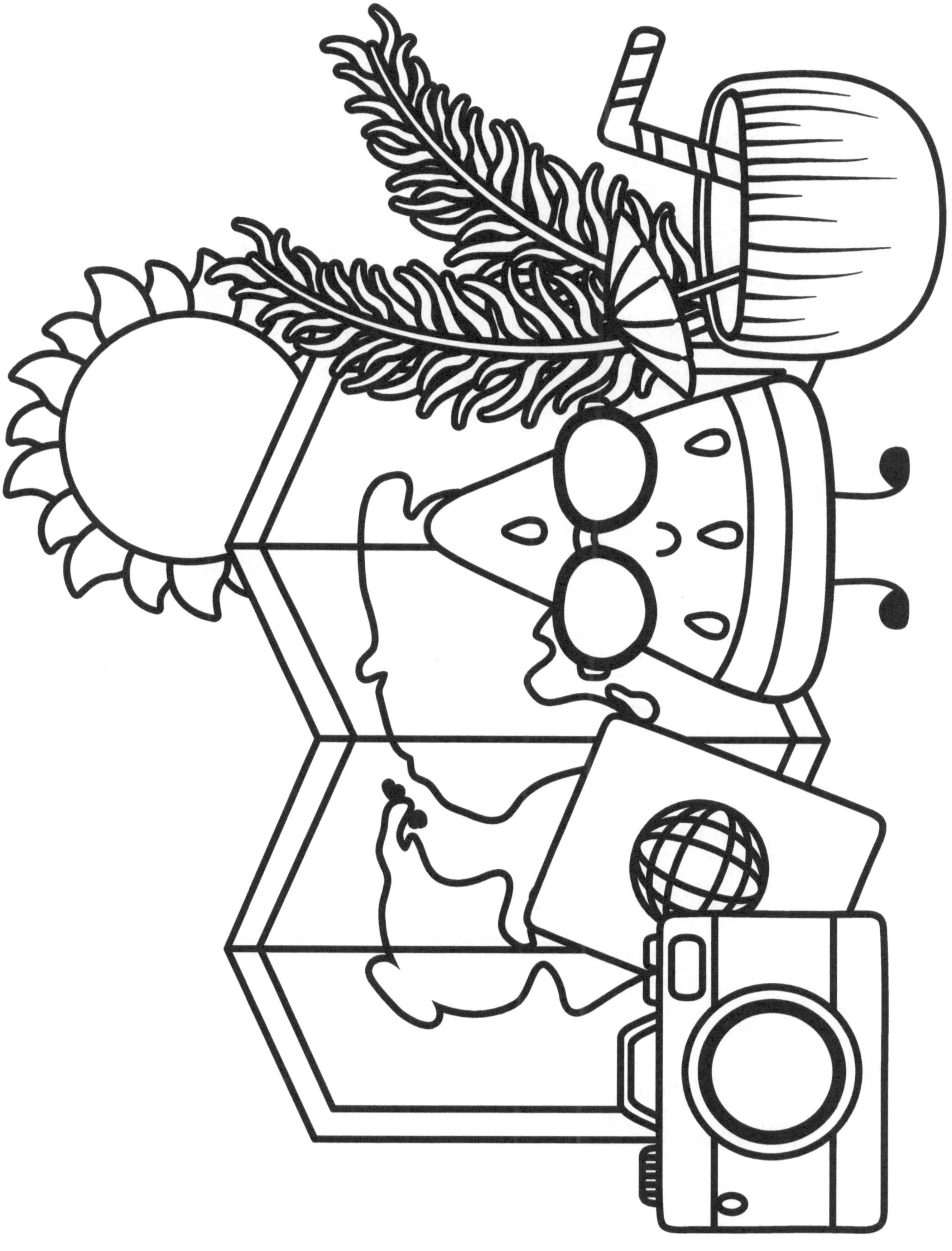

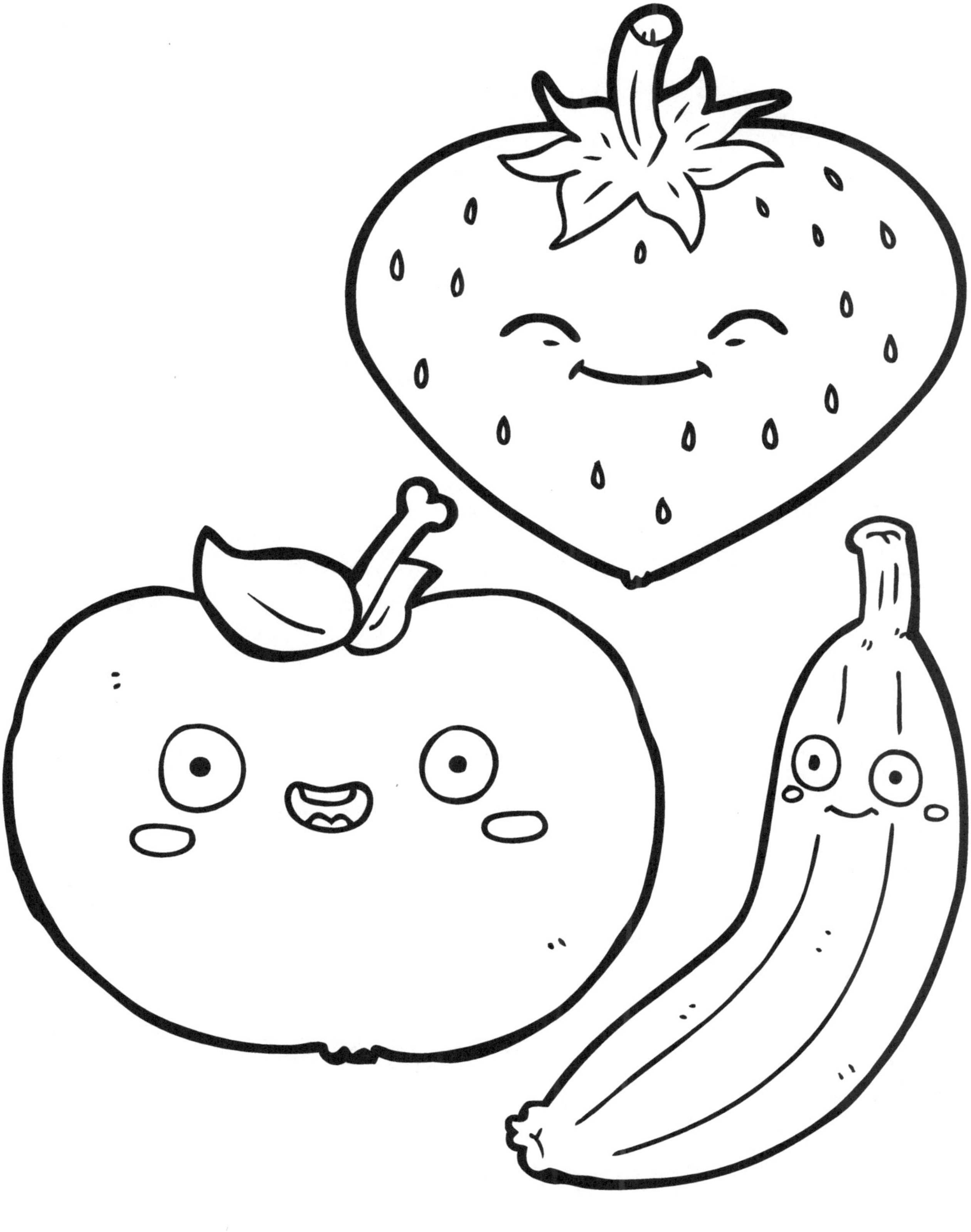

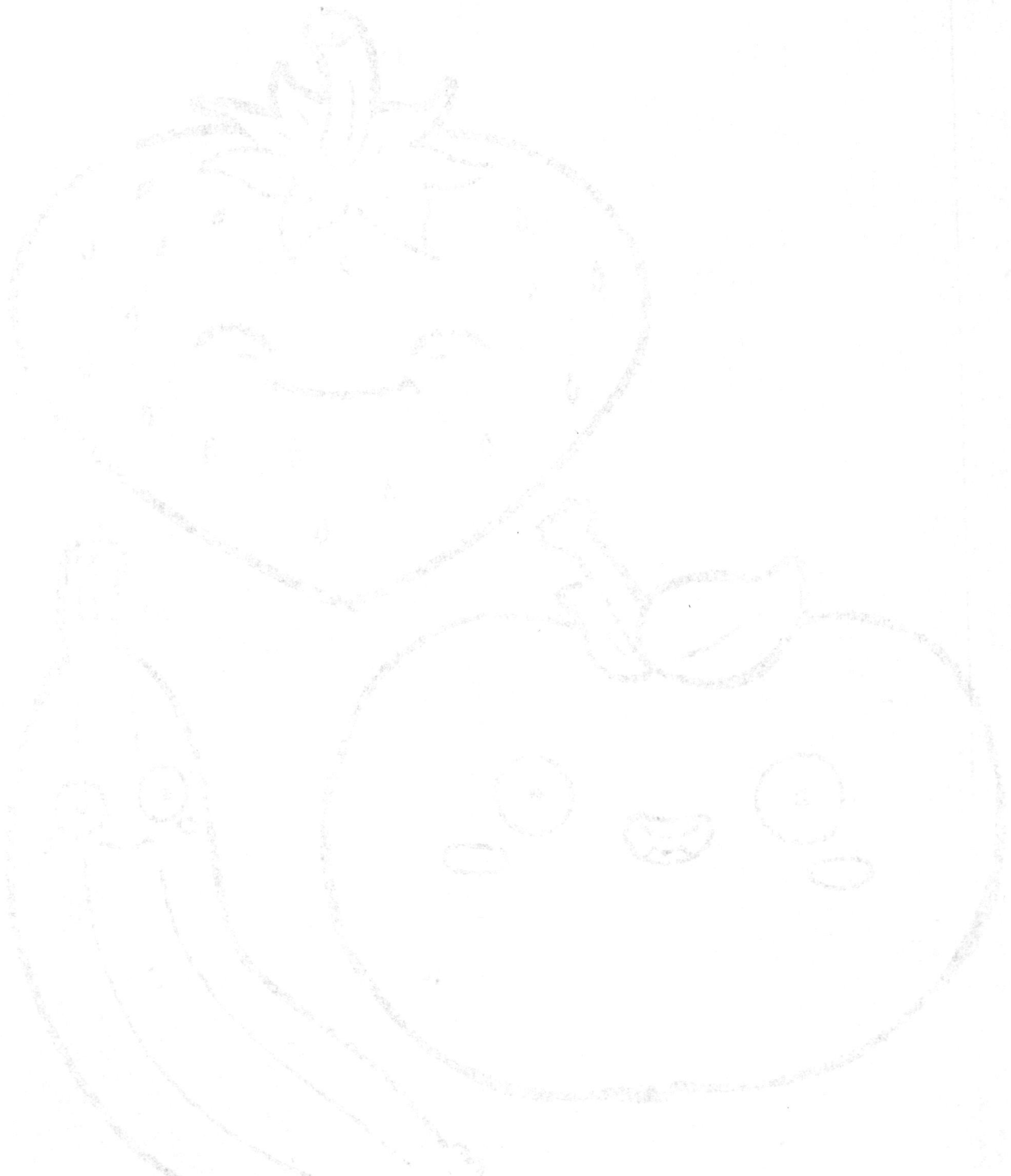

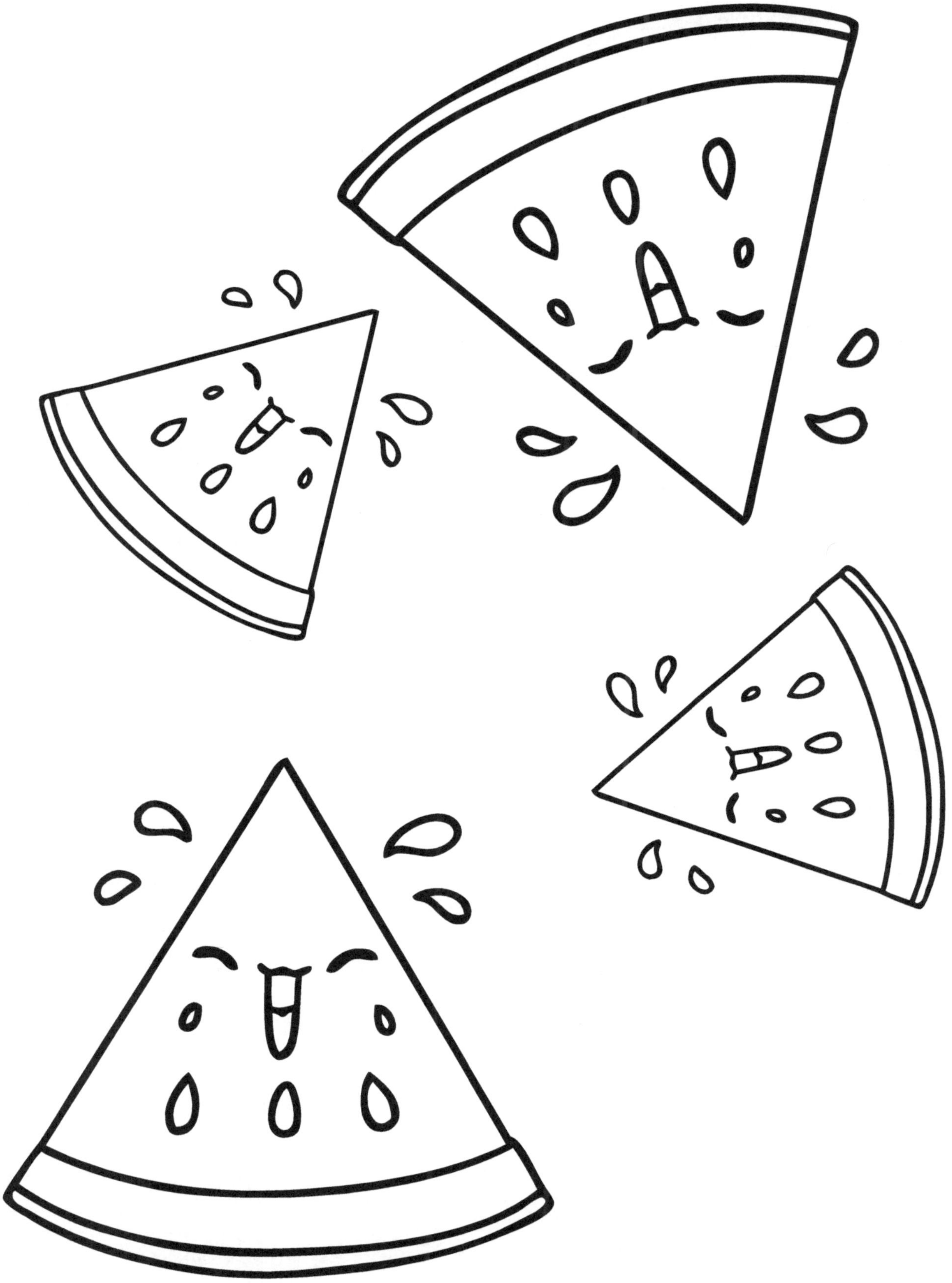

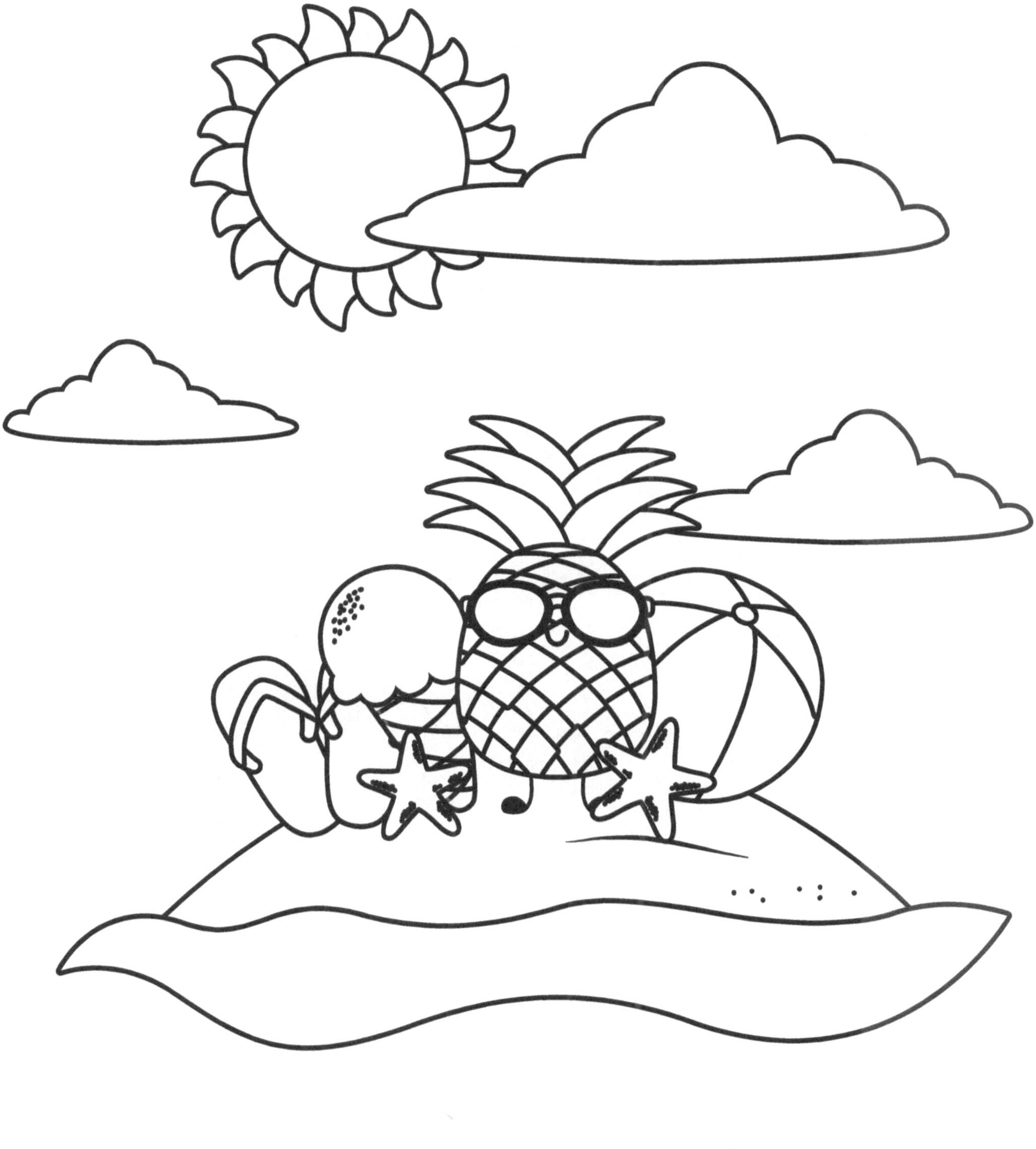

" I love colouring but i scratch" The cat Tom.

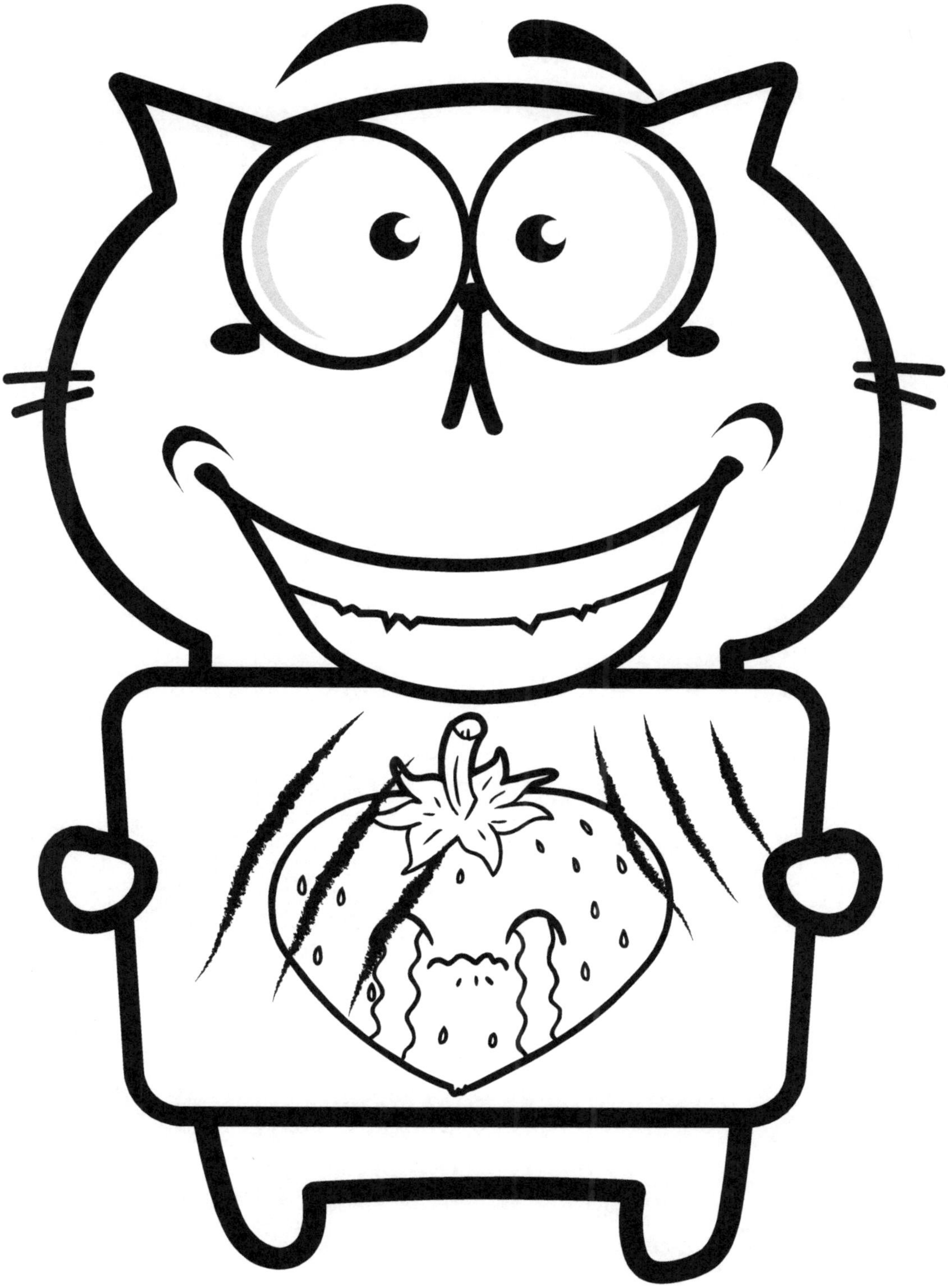

Made in United States
Troutdale, OR
09/26/2024

23164234R00058